FOOTPATHS OF BRITAIN
CENTRAL
ENGLAND

This is a Parragon Book
First published in 2003

Parragon
Queen Street House
4 Queen Street
Bath BA1 1HE
United Kingdom

Created and produced by
The Bridgewater Book Company Ltd,
Lewes, East Sussex

ISBN: 1-40540-502-3

Printed in China

www.walkingworld.com

Visit the Walkingworld website at www.walkingworld.com

All the walks in this book are available in more detailed form on the Walkingworld website. The route instructions have photographs at key decision points to help you to navigate, and each walk comes with an Ordnance Survey® map. Simply print them out on A4 paper and you are ready to go! A modest annual subscription gives you access to over 1,400 walks, all in this easy-to-follow format. If you wish, you can purchase individual walks for a small fee.

Next to every walk in this book you will see a Walk ID. You can enter this ID number on Walkingworld's 'Find a Walk' page and you will be taken straight to the details of that walk.

CONTENTS

Introduction

Britain is a fabulous place to walk. We are blessed with a varied and beautiful landscape, a dense network of public footpaths and places of historical interest at every corner. Add to all this the many thousands of well-placed pubs, tea shops and visitor attractions, and it's easy to see why walking is a treasured pastime for millions of people.

Walking is the perfect way to keep fit and healthy. It is good for your heart, muscles and body generally, without making the extreme demands of many sports. For most walkers, however, the health benefits are secondary. We walk for the sheer pleasure of it – being able to breathe in the fresh air, enjoy the company of our friends and 'get away from it all'.

Equipment

If you take up walking as a hobby, it is quite possible to spend a fortune on specialist outdoor kit. But you really don't need to. Just invest in a few inexpensive basics and you'll be ready to enjoy any of the walks in this book.

For footwear, boots are definitely best as they provide you with ankle support and protection from the inevitable mud, nettles and puddles. A light-weight pair should be fine if you have no intention of venturing up big hills or over rugged terrain. If you are not sure what to get, go to a specialist shop and ask for advice. Above all, choose boots that fit well and are comfortable.

Take clothing to deal with any weather that you may encounter. Allow for the 'wind-chill' factor – if your clothes get wet you will feel this cooling effect even more. Carry a small rucksack with a spare top, a hat and waterproofs, just in case. The key is being able to put on and take off layers of clothing at will and so keep an even, comfortable temperature throughout the day.

It's a good idea to carry some food and drink. Walking is exercise and you need to replace the fluid you lose through perspiration. Take a bottle of soft drink or water, and sip it regularly rather than downing it in one go. The occasional chocolate bar, sandwich or biscuit can work wonders when energy levels are flagging.

Walking poles – the modern version of the walking stick – are worth considering. They help you to balance and allow your arms to take some of the strain when going uphill. They also lessen the impact on your knees on downhill slopes. Don't be fooled into thinking that poles are just for the older walker – they are popular with trekkers and mountaineers of all ages.

Finding your way

Most walkers use Ordnance Survey® maps, rightly considered to be among the most accurate, up-to-date and 'walker–friendly' in the world. The 1:50,000 scale Landranger series has long been a favourite of outdoor enthusiasts. Almost all areas of Britain are also covered by the more detailed 1:25,000 scale Explorer and Explorer OL series. These include features such as field boundaries, farm buildings and small streams.

Having a map and compass – and learning how to use them – is vital to being safe in the countryside. Compass and map skills come with practice – there is no substitute for taking them out and having a go. Buy a compass with a transparent base plate and rotating dial; you will find this type in any outdoor shop. Most come with simple instructions – if not, ask in the shop for a guide.

If this all sounds a bit serious, I urge you not to worry too much about getting lost. We have all done it – some of us more often than we care to admit! You are unlikely to come to much harm unless you are on a featureless hilltop or out in very poor weather. If you want to build up your confidence, start with shorter routes through farmland or along the coastline and allow yourself plenty of time.

key to maps

Telephone
Start of route
Viewpoint
Pylon
Triangulation point
Radio mast
Church with Steeple
Church without Steeple
Chapel
Power
Golf course
Picnic area
Car park
Information
Lighthouse
Camping
Youth hostel
Bridge
Windmill
Highest point/summit
PH Public house
PC Public convenience
1666 Place of historical interest
Embankment/cutting
Rocky area/ sharp drop
Building
Castle
Tumulus
Garden

There are plenty of walks in this book that are perfect for the beginner. You can make navigating even easier by downloading the routes in this book from Walkingworld's website: www.walkingworld.com. These detailed walk instructions feature a photograph at each major decision point, to help you confirm your position and see where to go next.

Another alternative is to join a local walking group

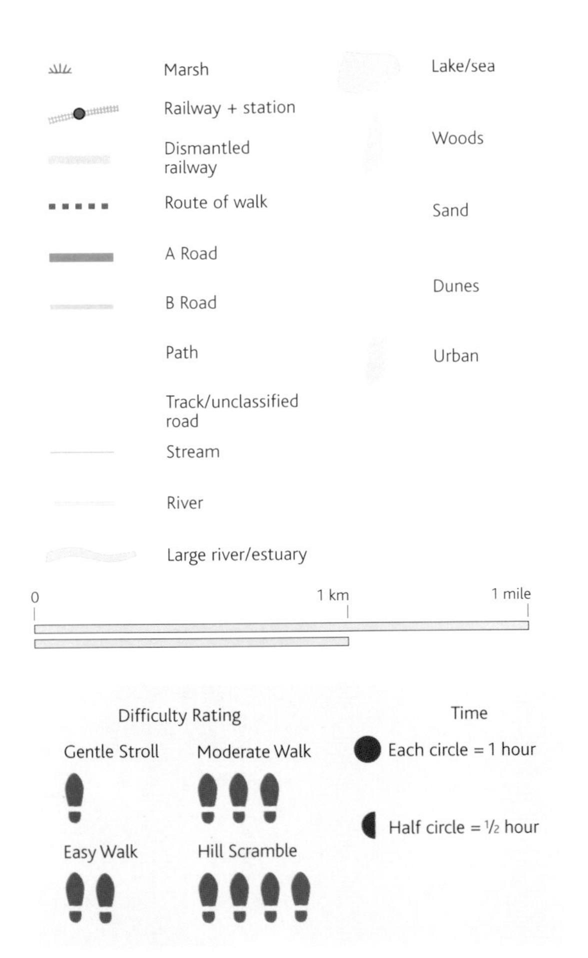

and learn from others. There are hundreds of such groups around the country, with members keen to share their experience and skills.

Enough words. Take the walks in this book as your inspiration. Grab your map and compass, and put on your boots. It's time to go out and walk!

Have fun.

David Stewart *Walkingworld*

▲ Map: Explorer 25
▲ Distance: 9.66 km/6 miles
▲ Walk ID: 812 Stephanie Kedik

Difficulty rating

Time

●●●

▲ Hills, Cliffs, Sea, Pub, Toilets, National Trust/NTS, Birds, Great Views, Gift Shop, Food Shop, Nature Trail, Tea Shop, Woodland

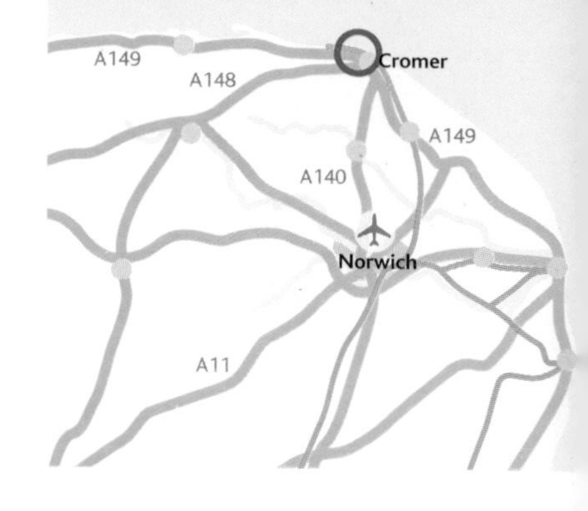

East and West Runton

This is a walk of great variety, centred around a beautiful part of the North Norfolk coast. The route takes in the pretty village of East Runton, beaches, woodland paths and stunning views from Beeston Regis cliffs.

❶ From the car park, turn right and go down to the beach. Turn left and walk along the beach, past a curious pointed rock formation, to some steep wooden steps. Climb the steps to the cliff top, turn right and walk across the camp site towards 'Beeston Bump'. Alternatively, follow the detour described in 'further information'.

❷ Leaving the camp site, turn left and follow the National Trail 'acorn' sign down a grassy track and across the level crossing. Cross the main road and take the lane to your left, towards 'The Roman Camp'. Follow the lane, which turns from shingle to dirt track, through Hall Farm and up to the woods.

❸ At the woods, turn left at the 'Beeston Regis Heath' sign. Where the track forks, follow the 'Coast Path' sign through a gate. Take the small footpath through the woods and go through another gate. At the junction, carry on through the woods, along a shingle track and past a caravan park. Carry on, following the larger shingle road round to your left.

❹ At a road junction, go straight across and take the 'acorn' path to your left. Pass a caravan site entrance and follow the bridleway to your right. At a junction of paths, take the bridleway towards Cromer. Go through a kissing gate, along the side of a field, through another gate and over a stream.

❺ Across the track, turn right, following the Coastal Path 'acorn' sign. Ignoring the two entrances to fields, take the small wooded track in the centre. Follow this through the trees to a farm track corner. Go straight down this track.

❻ At the junction with the road, turn left towards East Runton, past the village green and duck pond and round to your right. Continue under the viaducts and past the village sign. At the junction with the A149, turn right, cross over, and go down Beach Road to the car park.

further information

If you wish to avoid the steep steps in step 1, walk further along the beach to Sheringham. As you leave the beach and enter the town, head back along the cliff, over the hill called 'Beeston Bump', and reconnect with the walk at Step 2. This detour will add about 30–45 minutes to the walk. At high tide, the beach area can be stony, so walking shoes, or walking at low tide, are recommended. For tidal information, phone Cromer Tourist Information, 01263 512497.

access information

The Bittern Line runs from Norwich to the coast via Cromer and finishes at Sheringham, and also has an accessible station at West Runton (for information, phone Anglia Railways 01473 693333).

By car, West Runton can be reached via the A140 from Norwich/A149 coast road.

The walk begins at a 'pay-and-display' car park that operates every day, all year round.

For information on buses, phone NORBIC 0845 300 6116.

The imposing cliffs and grey waters of the North Norfolk coast provide the backdrop to a section of this varied walk.

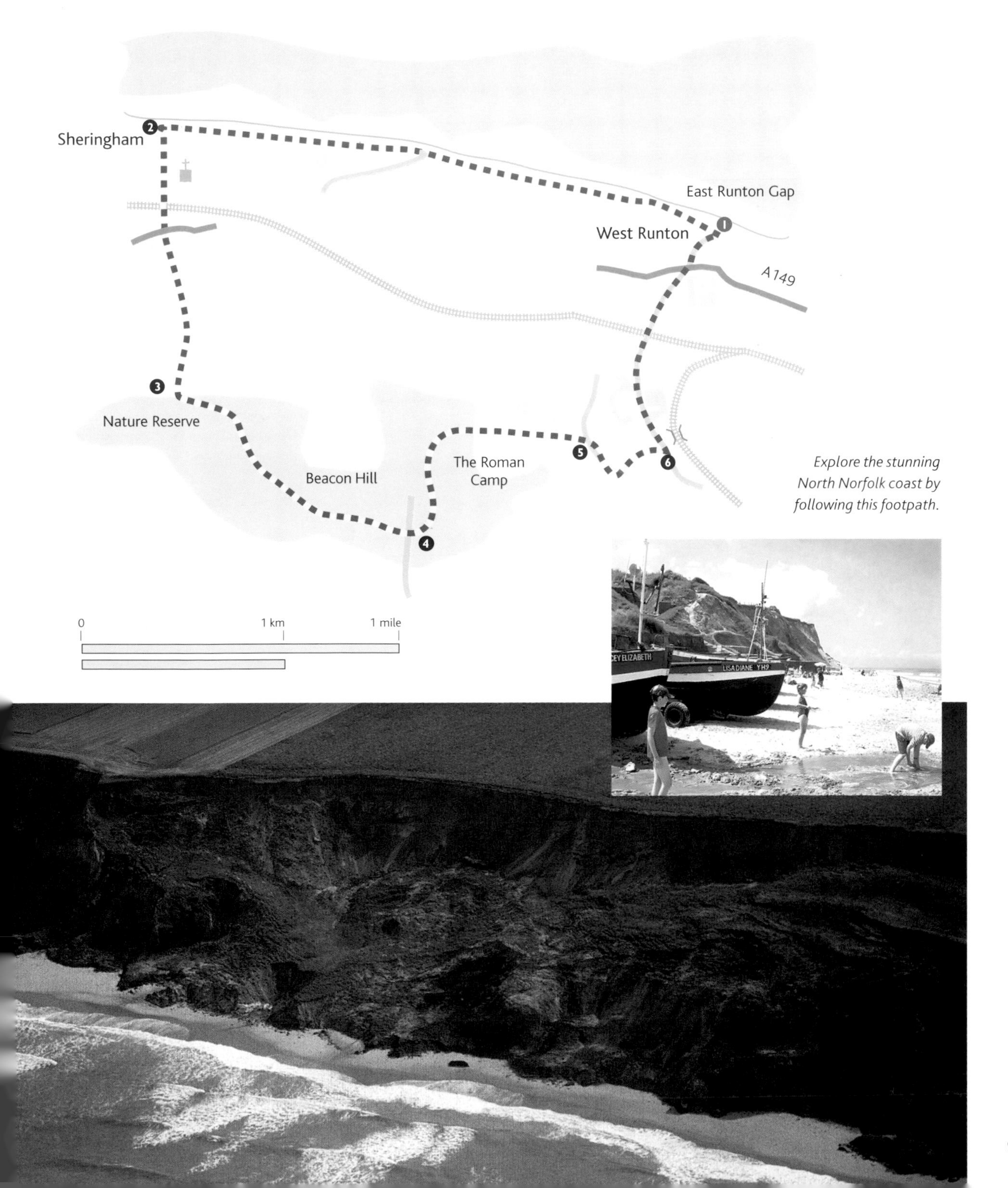

Explore the stunning North Norfolk coast by following this footpath.

▲ Map: Explorer 23
▲ Distance: 8.86 km/5½ miles
▲ Walk ID: 810 J. and C. Boldero

Difficulty rating

Time

▲ Sea, Pub, Toilets, Churches, Roman Fort, Wildlife, Birds, Flowers, Great Views, Butterflies

St Mary's Church, Burnham Deepdale.

Burnham Deepdale

This circular walk takes in part of the North Norfolk Coastal Path, passing tidal creeks with mussel beds and a wide variety of wading and sea birds. The return route passes the site of a 3rd-century Roman fort, then crosses Barrow Common.

❶ Starting with the garage on your left, walk along the road for a very short distance, then turn right along a No Through Road. Follow the signed footpath that runs between the trees. When you reach the finger signpost, turn left along the coastal path, with the creeks on your right. Follow this winding path to the end at Brancaster Staithe, where you pass between brick sheds by a cottage.

❷ Turn left along the track, then almost immediately right, following the yellow arrow on the wall. Go along a narrow path between a fence and a brick wall, then through a gate. Follow the board walk to the end at Brancaster.

❸ Turn left along a country lane, then at the main road turn left again by the church, with the Ship Inn opposite. Turn left along London Road, then right along the narrow lane just before the last house on the right (if you reach a footpath, you have gone too far). At the end of the lane, turn right along the gravel path, then left along a country lane, following the path round the site of the Roman fort.

❹ When you reach the main road, cross it and turn left along the pavement, which is hidden between the grass and the hedge. Almost immediately, turn right up a wide, hedged track, and at the top turn right again along a grassy track.

❺ Go through the gate on to Barrow Common, ignoring the path on the left. When you reach the open space, keep to the right-hand path, which later veers left with the wood on the right. At the country lane, turn right for a very short distance, then left along another country lane. At the T-junction in Burnham Deepdale, turn right to the lay-by and the start of the walk.

access information

There is a coastal bus route (for information, phone Freephone 0500 626116, Monday to Saturday, 8.30 a.m. to 5 p.m.). There is parking in the long lay-by opposite the garage and by the church at Burnham Deepdale, which is situated on the A149, 11.25 km west of Wells-next-the-Sea in North Norfolk.

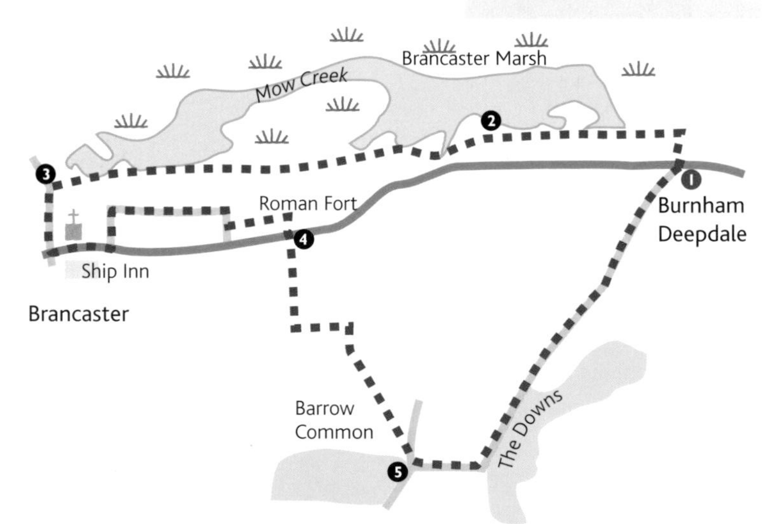

further information

Burnham Deepdale Church has an Anglo-Saxon tower and a font with a Normal bowl. At St Mary's in Brancaster, look out for a carving of a man with his head at a very strange angle. Brancaster Staithe has been a fishing port since Roman times.

0 1 km 1 mile

▲ Map: Explorer OL 40

▲ Distance: 5.5 km/3½ miles

▲ Walk ID: 800 Stephanie Kedik

Difficulty rating

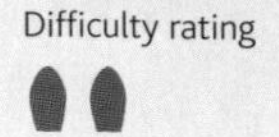

Time

▲ River, Pub, Toilets, Play Area, Church, Wildlife, Birds, Flowers, Butterflies, Gift Shop, Food Shop, Good for Kids, Nature Trail, Tea Shop

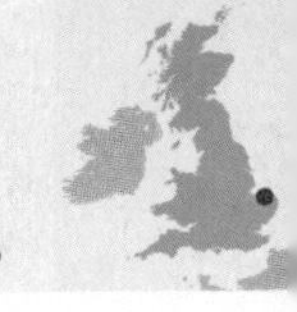

Ludham Marshes

access information

Ludham can be reached by car from Norwich (A1151/A1062) or by bus (for information, phone Norfolk Bus Information on 0845 300 6116).

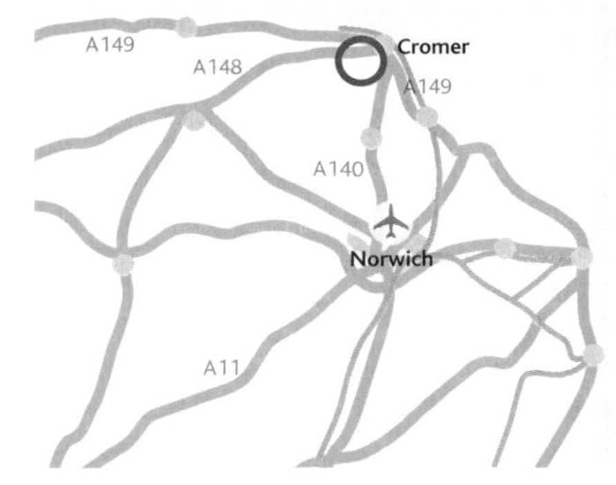

This picturesque stroll starts in the beautiful village of Ludham and takes in Ludham Marshes Nature Reserve. Renowned for their abundance of wildlife, the marshes sit alongside the River Thurne, where boatyards are dotted along the banks.

❶ From the centre of Ludham, take the main Yarmouth Road past the Ludham village sign at Bakers Arms Green. Further down, on the right, is a little path leading off and running alongside the road. Follow this until you reach a right turn where Horse Fen Road meets the Yarmouth Road.

❷ Turn right into Horse Fen Road. Continue along the lane, past Womack Water boat hire and camp site. Follow the public bridleway down on to Ludham Marshes National Nature Reserve.

❸ As you take the path round the corner and into the reserve, you will pass first a garden and then a wood on your left beyond the drainage ditch (deer are sometimes seen in the wood). On your right, the marshes stretch out across to the River Thurne. Follow the footpath through the reserve.

❹ Where you meet the gravel track, take a turn to the right through the gate (which says 'Danger – Unstable road!'). Continue along this track and go through another gate.

❺ When you reach Horse Fen pumping station, turn right to follow the green footpath sign. Across the bridge, follow the footpath along the river, keeping the river on your left. Although this stretch can be a bit overgrown in summer, it is compensated by the views of the river.

❻ Follow the footpath back from the river, up the creek, and out of the reserve at the side of Hunters Yard. Walk back up Horse Fen Road, past Womack Water and the boatyard. At the top of Horse Fen Road, turn left and follow the road leading back into Ludham village.

The marshes are renowned for their wildlife and provide a peaceful environment for sailors of small craft.

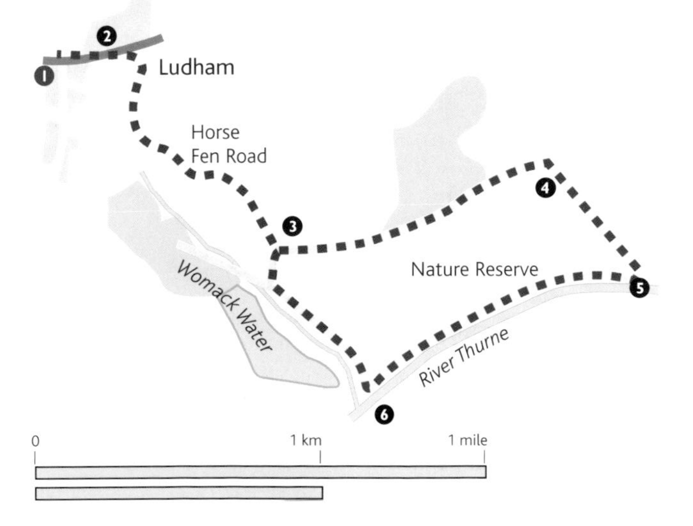

further information

In the summer months Ludham Marshes Nature Reserve buzzes with insects and butterflies, and there are many varieties of birds to be seen all year round. Deer are also sometimes spotted in the nearby wood. The undergrowth along the riverbank can grow quite high, so leg-covering is recommended. Boats can be hired by the day from the marina in the village.

▲ Map: Explorer OL 40
▲ Distance: 12.08 km/7½ miles
▲ Walk ID: 1372 J. and C. Boldero

Difficulty rating

Time

▲ River, Pub, Toilets, Wildlife, Birds, Great Views, Food Shop

Halvergate Marshes

This walk through Halvergate Marshes follows tracks and crosses meadows, passing Breydon Water and running alongside the River Yare. The marshes have a unique and very special atmosphere, desolate in summer and even more so in winter.

1 From where you parked your car, walk along the tarmac lane, which becomes a rough track. Follow the track as it winds along, going through gates and over stiles until you reach a concrete lane.

2 Turn right along the concrete track marked 'Weavers Way' and continue to follow it to the railway crossing. Cross the lines with care. With the building on your right, keep right until you reach a stile and a notice-board.

3 Climb the stile and turn left along the bank, with Breydon Water on your left. Continue to follow the path, passing the Berney Arms pub and windmill on your right.

4 At the windmill, turn right down the steps, climb the stile, and continue along the gravel path. Turn left to two white posts by the sign 'Railway Station'. Go through the gate and cross the meadow, aiming for the white gates ahead.

5 At the railway station, cross the lines, then go through the gate, turn right over the stile, and turn left across the meadow. Continue across the meadows, going through or over the gates. The ditch is now on your right. When you reach the gate with a 'Weavers Way' sign on it, go through it.

6 Go over the earth bridge on your right, then turn left along the grass track. Climb the stile and cross the meadows to the barriers ahead. Continue through or over more gates and over another earth bridge. Climb the next stile and continue along the path heading towards the windmill, where the path goes left. Go through a small gate, and continue along the path. Go round to the stile, climb it, then turn left to return to your car.

access information

By car, from the A47 turn off to Halvergate 4 km/2½ miles east of Acle. At the right-hand bend, turn left at the Weavers Way sign along a tarmac lane, and park on the verge just after passing farm buildings. By train, go by Anglia Railways to Berney Arms station, and follow the walk route from Step 5 (for information, phone 0845 748 4950, a 24-hour service, or local call Norwich 01603 764776, open daily 8 a.m. to 10 p.m.).

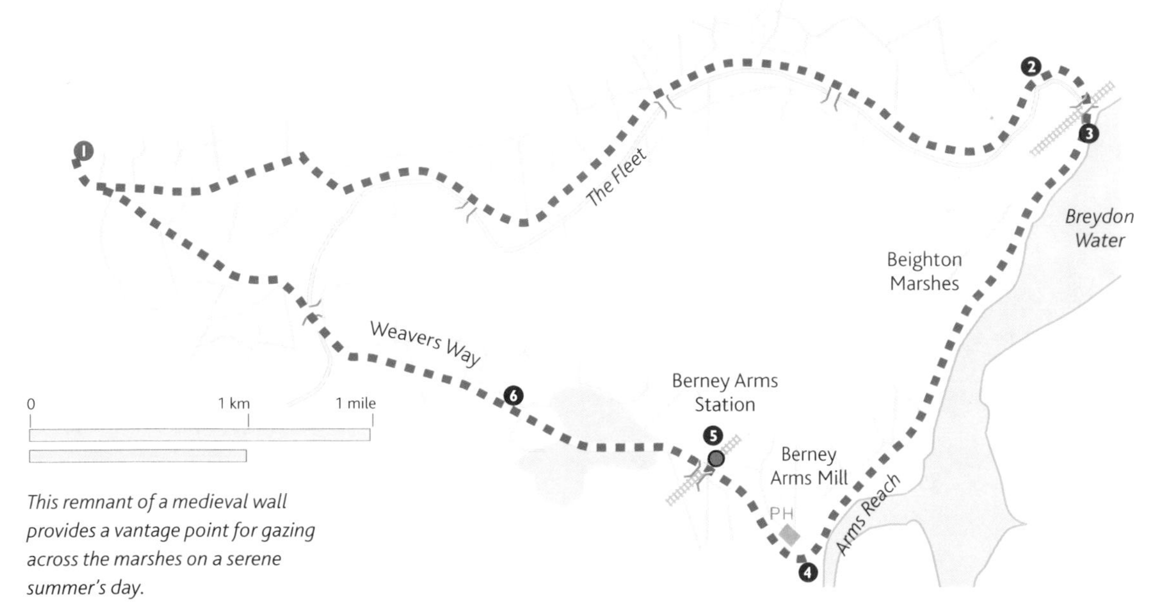

This remnant of a medieval wall provides a vantage point for gazing across the marshes on a serene summer's day.

This walk leads to the most charming riverside views along the River Yare.

further information

The Berney Arms windmill, built in the 1800s for the Berney family, is said to be the finest and tallest on the Broads, and is usually open to the public. Cattle and sheep graze on Halvergate Marshes, so dogs should be kept on leads.

▲ Map: Explorer 212
▲ Distance: 14.49 km/9 miles
▲ Walk ID: 641 B. and A. Sandland

Difficulty rating

Time

▲ Pub, Toilets, Play Area, National Trust/NTS, Wildlife, Birds, Flowers, Great Views, Accessible for Wheelchairs

Sizewell and Minsmere from Dunwich

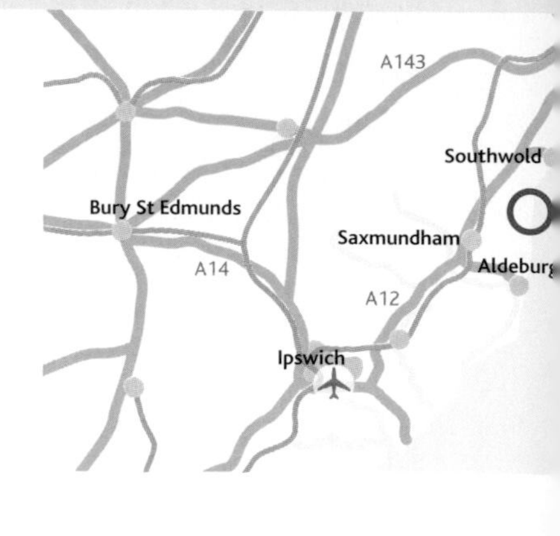

This walk from Dunwich crosses heath and woodland, passing through Eastbridge before taking in the majestic forest of Sizewell Belts. An alternative is to visit the dazzling dome of the Sizewell Power Station, before returning via the seashore.

❶ From the car park, go through the gap between the pine trees to the right of the toilets. Follow this wide track left over the heath (do not take the track which rises to the right). Continue until you enter woodland at a stile.

❷ Climb the stile and continue in the same direction. At a T-junction of tracks, turn left. When you reach a narrow road, cross straight over and carry on, with fields to both sides of the track.

❸ Enter more woodland and descend to meet another narrow road on a bend. Go straight ahead along the road, bearing left at a house. Cross the bridge over the Minsmere, and keep going, passing the Eel's Foot on your left.

❹ Continue along the road to a footpath on the left, leading to an abandoned cottage. At the cottage, turn right along a broad track between hedges. Follow the track gently downhill, then up again.

❺ At the belt of trees on your left, look for a wide gate and a stile. Climb the stile and follow the track through the left-hand edge of the trees. When the trees become denser on the left, you begin to descend slightly. At the bottom, bear right along the main track, following the black arrow on a post.

❻ Continue, following two more black arrows close to each other. Another black arrow sends you right at a fork. The track suddenly veers left, away from the power station, and here you turn right at another black arrow. Go over two bridges and a wooden walkway. At the next black arrow, turn left and follow the path to the end of the mound on your right. At the large concrete blocks, turn left along a wide grass track. Follow this path, parallel to the sea, all the way back to the car park at Dunwich.

access information

Take the unclassified road eastwards off the A12, just north-east of Yoxford, signposted to Westleton/Dunwich. In Westleton, turn left along the B1125 signposted Blythburgh/ Dunwich, then after 100 m take the turn right signposted Minsmere/Dunwich. Follow signs to Dunwich Heath (right after the track to Mount Pleasant Farm on the right). Park in the National Trust car park.

further information

In addition to the visitor centre at Sizewell, there are plenty of places of interest in this area, including Dunwich Heath, owned by the National Trust; the small village of Dunwich, which was once a large and influential town and now lies mostly below the sea; and the renowned RSPB reserve at Minsmere.

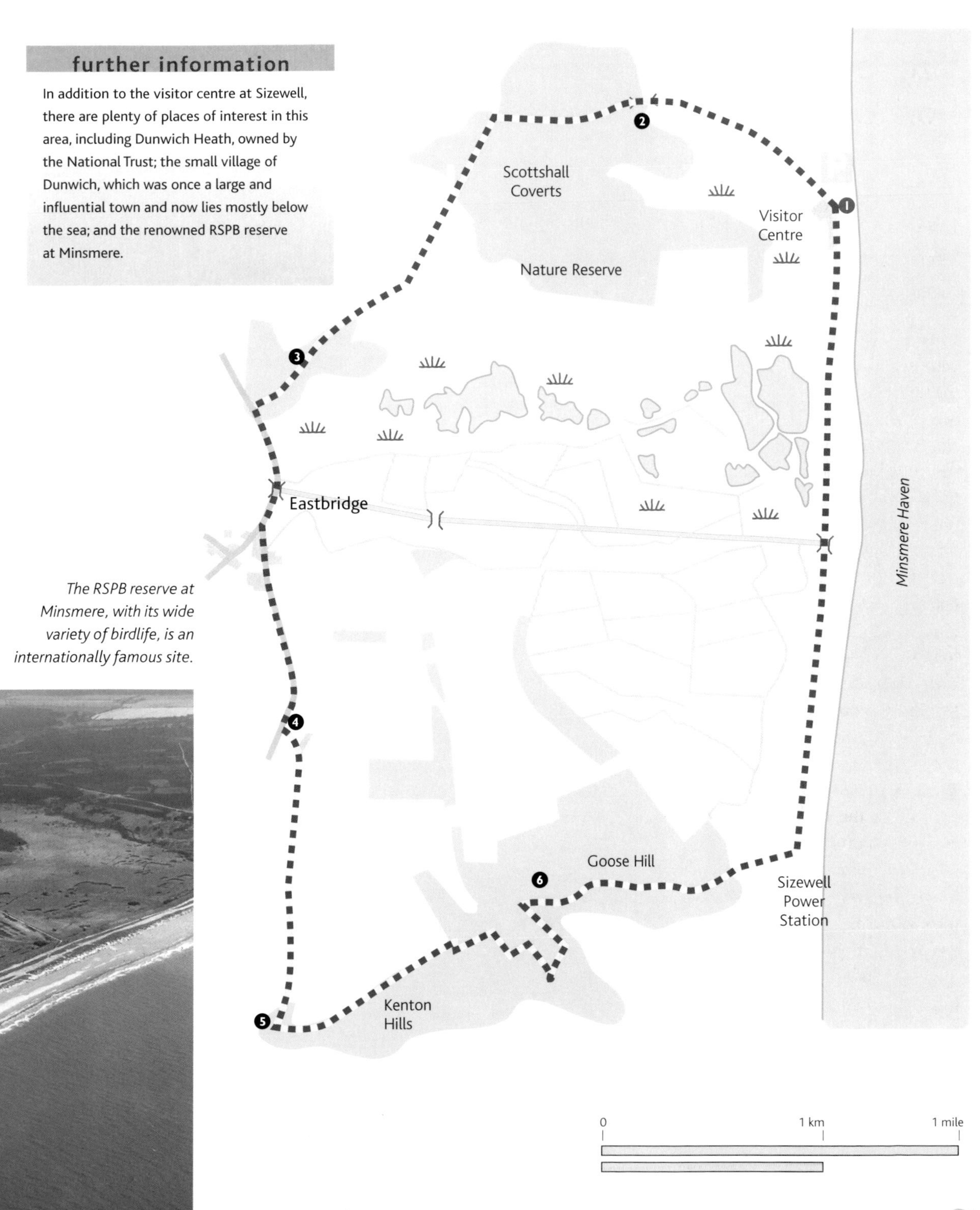

The RSPB reserve at Minsmere, with its wide variety of birdlife, is an internationally famous site.

▲ Map: Explorer 212
▲ Distance: 11.27 km/7 miles
▲ Walk ID: 1359 B. and A. Sandland

Difficulty rating ●●

Time ●●●

▲ Sea, Pub, Toilets, Museum, Play Area, Church, Castle, National Trust/NTS, Birds, Great Views, Good for Kids, Restaurant, Tea Shop, Ancient Monument

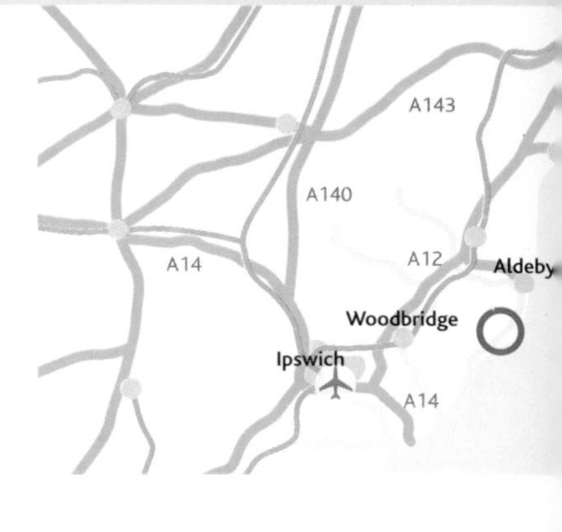

Orford and the Rivers Ore and Butley

This walk is perfect for experiencing the vastness of the sky and seascapes of East Anglia. There are superb views of Orford Ness and Havergate Island across the River Ore, and the route takes in a medieval castle at Orford.

❶ From the car park, walk to the quay, then turn right and soon bear right again. Climb the steps to the river bank. Turn left and follow the path along the bank. When you reach the Butley River, turn inland with it, climbing another stile but still on the raised bank. Continue past the ferry landing then cross another stile near some huts. Soon after, descend to a track on your right.

❷ Carry on along the track with a paddock on your left, then a cottage on your right. The track then turns left and right. Continue to follow it, passing Gedgrave Hall on your left. Just before Richmond Farm, take the path to the left by the postbox.

❸ Just before the track bends to the right, take a signposted path right. After climbing the steps, enter a field. The path ahead crosses several fields, heading straight for Orford Castle. Cross a drive and continue ahead.

❹ At the castle, carry on to the road, then on the road head for the church. By the King's Head, go slightly left to enter the churchyard. Keeping the church porch on your left, go right to another gate and exit the churchyard, turning left on a road.

❺ Continue on this road to Brundish Lane. Follow Brundish Lane, bearing right at a junction then turning right again at a T-junction after the Rectory on your left. Just before a large house with a high brick wall, turn left on to a signposted track.

❻ After the gate, follow the grass path which heads initially for the lighthouse. At the end of a deep ditch on the right, bear half right to cross a field. At the far side, cross a stile and climb steps to the river bank. Follow the path back to your starting point.

access information

From the A12 (London to Great Yarmouth), turn on to the A1152 at Woodbridge. Just after Wilford Bridge, take the B1084, signposted to Orford. In Orford, park in the pay-and-display car park near the quay.

The route provides superb views of Orford Ness across the River Ore.

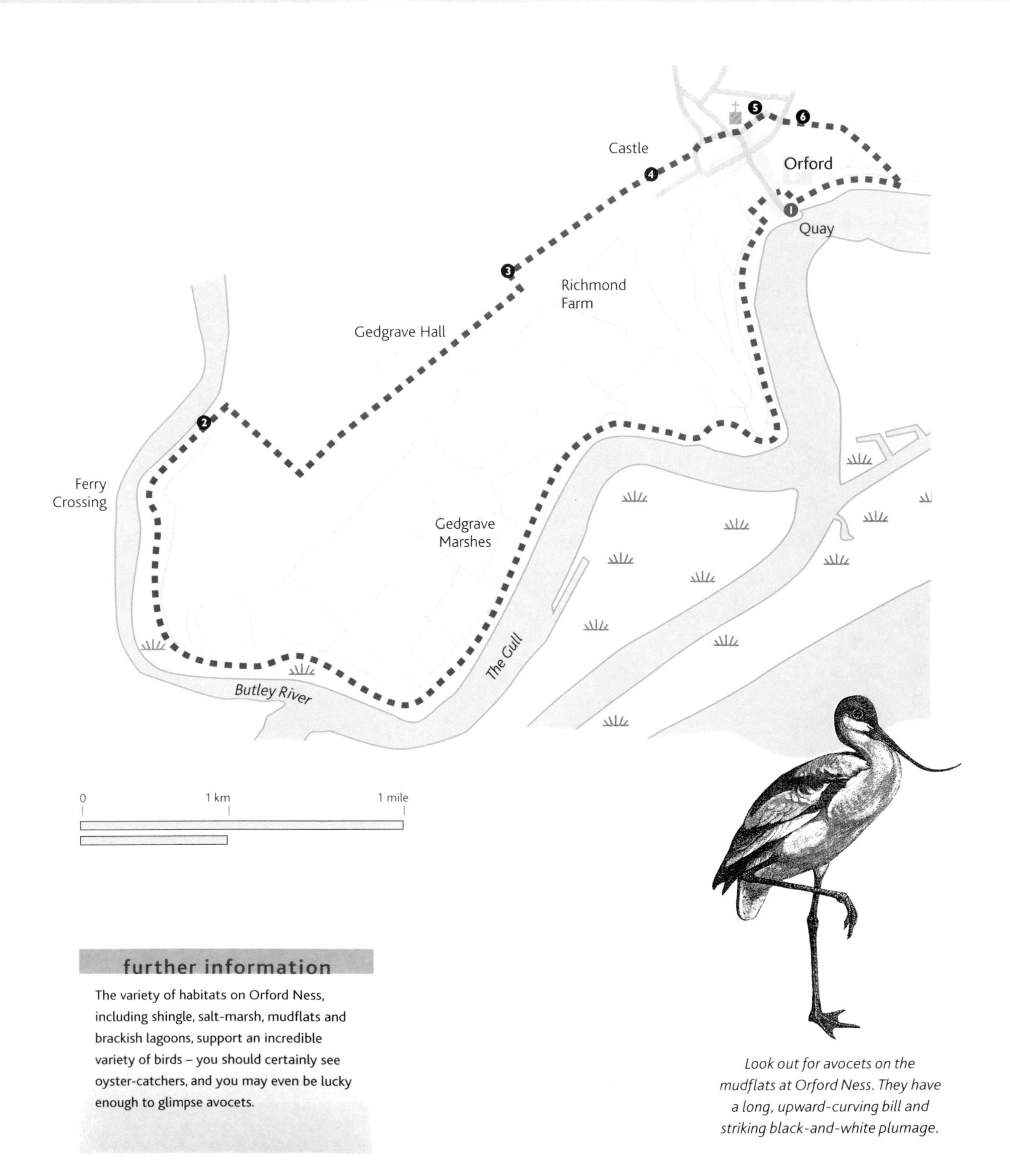

further information

The variety of habitats on Orford Ness, including shingle, salt-marsh, mudflats and brackish lagoons, support an incredible variety of birds – you should certainly see oyster-catchers, and you may even be lucky enough to glimpse avocets.

Look out for avocets on the mudflats at Orford Ness. They have a long, upward-curving bill and striking black-and-white plumage.

▲ Map: Explorer 225
▲ Distance: 9 km/5½ miles
▲ Walk ID: 106 Nicholas Rudd-Jones

Difficulty rating

Time

▲ River, Pub, Mill, National Trust Tea Room, Picnic Site, Nature Reserve, Museum, Good for Kids

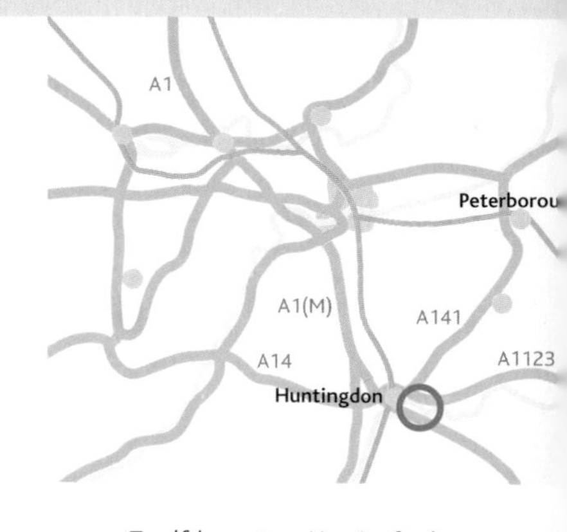

St Ives and Hemingford Grey from Hemingford Abbots

This is a charming riverside walk in the Cambridgeshire fens, taking in the delightful villages of Hemingford Abbots and Hemingford Grey as well as the historic town of St Ives. If time permits, there is a working flour mill and a nature reserve in an ancient osier bed to visit en route.

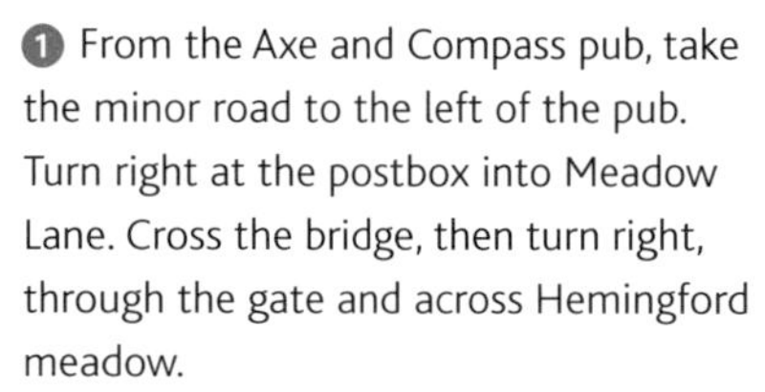

❶ From the Axe and Compass pub, take the minor road to the left of the pub. Turn right at the postbox into Meadow Lane. Cross the bridge, then turn right, through the gate and across Hemingford meadow.

❷ Cross the bridge over the lock, then turn left and over the rollers, heading right on the tarmac path. Turn left over a small bridge to Houghton Mill. Follow the Ouse Valley Way footpath sign. Go through the gates and turn right along the gravel path.

❸ Passing the National Trust Tea Room on the right, follow the yellow waymarks across the field, past the caravan site. Carry on until you reach a kissing gate on your left. Go through, then turn right along the gravel path by a brick wall. At the junction, turn left and then right along a minor road.

further information

Houghton Mill is open weekends and bank holidays April–September, 2–5.30 p.m. Punts are available for hire at weekends 10 a.m.–6 p.m. and weekdays during school holidays 2–6 p.m. For info, phone 01480 468184. Holt Island Nature Reserve is open on Sundays April–September 10.30 a.m.– 5 p.m. At other times, phone 01480 388500.

Twelfth-century Hemingford Grey Manor is reputedly the oldest continuously inhabited house in Britain.

4 As the tarmac road swings left, take a small footbridge across the river and follow this road. Pass through St Ives thicket, emerging by the river. At the next junction, go straight ahead (signposted 'Ouse Valley Way'). The path continues through gardens, coming out opposite the church.

5 Go through the churchyard and out via the iron gates. Follow the road to the Jubilee monument and fork right. Turn right at the end of the road and cross the town bridge. Take the first right turn, following the footpath to Hemingford Grey. Go through a gate and cross the meadows on the left-hand path.

6 Go through the gate and join a track. Immediately, take the path to the left to join a road. At the next junction, take the footpath straight ahead. Turn right at the road, then left on to the footpath by the church. Follow the path back to the village. At the road, turn right and return to the Axe and Compass.

Houghton Mill is a major historic attraction along the route of this walk.

access information

Hemingford Abbots is just off the A14 from Huntingdon to Cambridge, between the junctions for Huntingdon and St Ives.

Wyton
Mill
Black Bridge
PH
Hemingford Abbots
Hemingford Grey
St Ives
0
1 km
1 mile

▲ Map: Explorer 227
▲ Distance: 10 km/6¼ miles
▲ Walk ID: 38 Nicholas Rudd-Jones

Difficulty rating

Time

▲ Steam Train, Country Park, Model Train Rides, Lake, River, Boat Trips in Summer, Toilets, Museum, Play Area, Wildlife, Birds, Flowers, Great Views

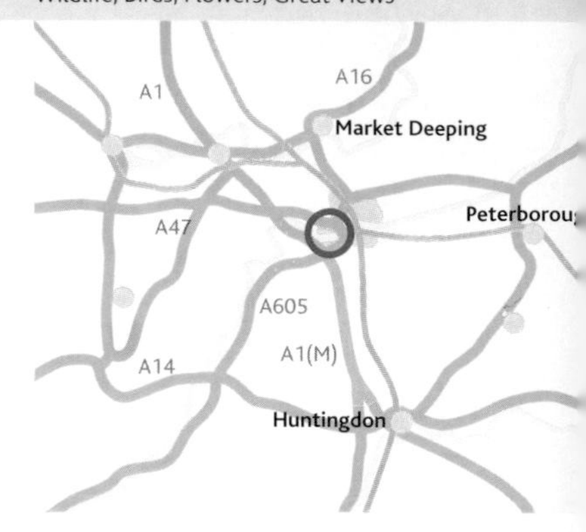

Nene Valley Railway & Ferry Meadows

Take a nostalgic trip on the Nene Valley Railway, a preserved steam train running from Wansford to Ferry Meadows, then walk back to Wansford through an area of great historic interest, following the meandering River Nene.

❶ From the station, follow the platform towards the level crossing. Cross the road and take the path between the trees to the left. Follow the path by the driveway into Ferry Meadows Country Park. Walk either side of Overton Lake and cross the bridge at the far corner.

❷ Turn left at the junction and follow the path by Gunwade Lake. At the next junction, take the right path, bearing left by the river. Turn right over the ferry bridge. Immediately turn left, go through the gate and follow the path by the river.

❸ At the junction with Landy Green Way, continue alongside the river to the railway bridge. At the Nene Valley Railway bridge, take the steep path up to the railway track and cross over, back to the riverside path.

❹ The footpath is blocked here, so cross the first footbridge and return over the second. At the old mill follow Mill Road, turning left at the footpath sign on to a narrow fenced path. Climb the stile and follow the track beside the fence. Climb the next stile, and turn left across the field to the footbridge.

❺ Cross the bridge and the field to the right of the oxbow lake. Then follow the path by the river. Cross another bridge and pass a row of pollarded trees. Climb the stile and cross a third footbridge. Go past the bridge to Water Newton, pass the gate and stile and carry on.

❻ At a small weir, climb the stile waymarked 'Nene Way', and follow the edge of the field. At the corner, turn right towards the pylon. Climb the stile and follow the field edge, parallel to the railway track. Climb another stile and carry on. At Wansford station, go down the wooden steps, turn right and follow the path to the bridge.

The meandering course of the River Nene accompanies the walker along most of this route.

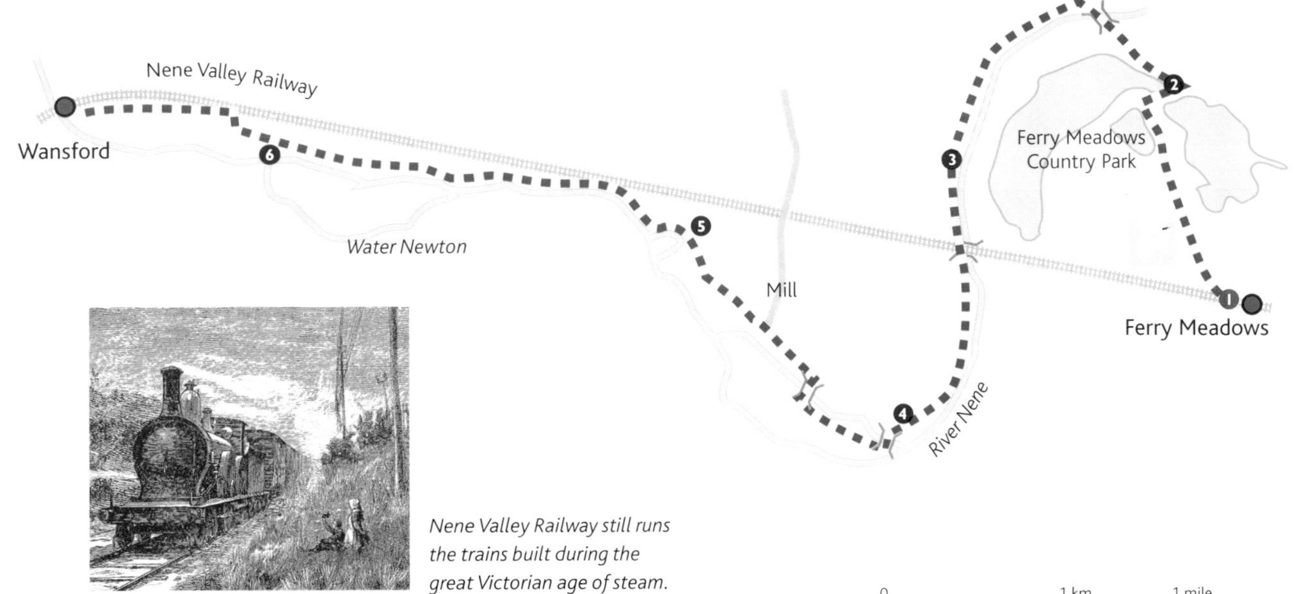

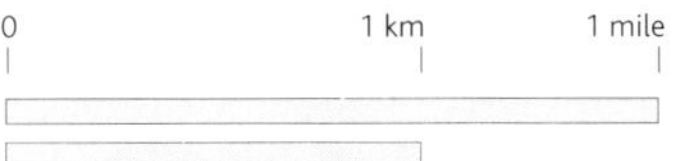

Nene Valley Railway still runs the trains built during the great Victorian age of steam.

access information

Wansford Station is situated at a turning off the A1, just south of Wansford. Stagecoach bus no 367 from Peterborough runs to the station.

further information

For train information, phone the Talking Timetable on 01780 784404 for times, or 01780 784444 for ticket prices and further information; or go to the website http://www.uel.ac.uk/pers/1278/rly-pres/nene.html

For a longer walk, take the train to Orton Mere, cross at Orton Lock and walk along the north bank of the River Nene to Bluebell Bridge, rejoining the walk at Overton Lake.

▲ Map: Explorer 245
▲ Distance: 8.75 km/5½ miles
▲ Walk ID: 647 Jude Howat

Difficulty rating

Time

▲ Canal, River, Pubs, Wildlife, Birds, Great Views

Aston-on-Trent and Trent & Mersey Canal

This delightful circular walk begins on good towpaths by the Trent and Mersey Canal, then crosses over open land to follow a small section of the River Derwent before returning to the canal path.

❶ From the lay-by, head down the track towards the canal. Cross over the bridge and follow the towpath to the left. Shortly after passing a pub on the opposite side, the path runs closer to the canal bank. Go under a bridge and carry on to a lock just before a high bridge over the River Trent.

❷ Go on to the bridge to see the canal merging with the rivers Trent and Derwent, then retrace your steps to the lock and very carefully cross the canal. On the far side, follow a footpath leading from the canal to the River Derwent. After passing between two ponds, the path becomes unclear, but aim towards the large tree by the river.

❸ At the tree, the path becomes clear again. Follow the riverbank until you reach the first bridge. Do not cross the bridge, but turn left and follow the path across the fields towards the houses, to a metalled track.

❹ Join the metalled road and follow it round a sharp bend and past a converted church. Turn right off this road just before a bridge over the canal. Aim towards a white pub in the distance. Just after the pub, the road bends sharply to the left. Follow the road to reach a small lane off to the right.

❺ Go through the lane, then follow the road on the far side. When you reach a T-junction, turn right. At this point, you can see the pub you passed earlier on the walk. Cross the road and go through the pub car park and to the left of the building to the canal.

❻ Carefully cross the canal via one of the locks. Turn right at the far side, and follow the canal towpath back to the start of the walk.

A barge progresses sedately along the calm waters of the Trent and Mersey Canal as it makes its way through the peaceful countryside to its junction with the Trent and Derwent rivers.

access information

Aston-on-Trent is just south of the A50 between Derby and Nottingham. There is lay-by parking close to the start of the walk, and also a community centre car park nearby.

further information

As long as they are closely supervised, this is a good route for young children – the towpath is easy to walk, and there are usually fishermen sitting on the banks, with all kinds of fascinating grubs squirming in tins! The path between the canal and the river can get quite damp after rain, so wellies and old clothes are recommended for little people who enjoy jumping in puddles.

The canal route is well-served by pubs like this one, typically built right at the water's edge.

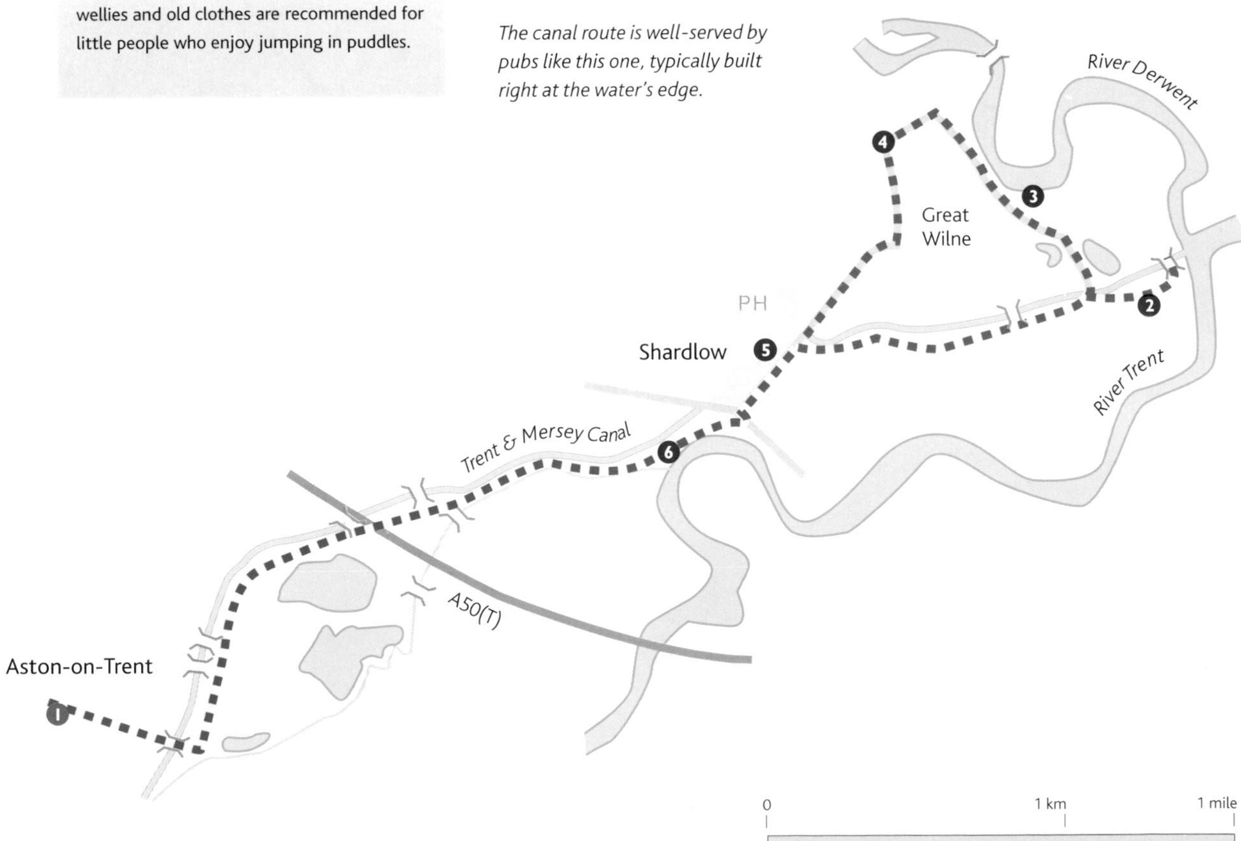

▲ Map: Explorer 15
▲ Distance: 4.19 km/2½ miles
▲ Walk ID: 65 Nicholas Rudd-Jones

Difficulty rating

Time

▲ River, Pub, Toilets, Museum, Church, Wildlife, Birds, Flowers, Great Views

The River Welland.

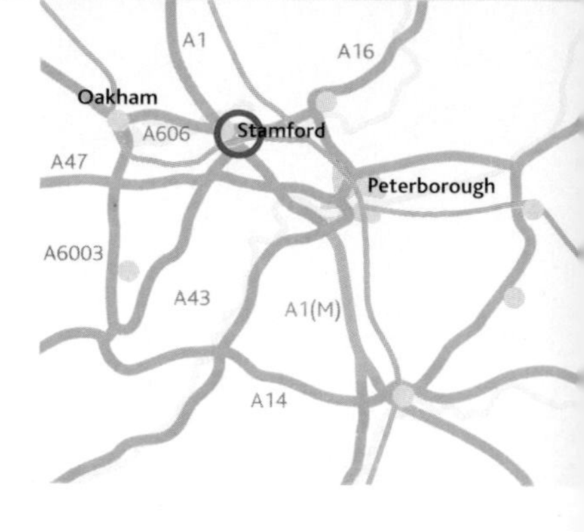

Stamford to the end of the meadows and back

This short, easy walk captures all the magic of the meadows, and gives a splendid view of the town. History lovers can relish standing on the spot where the feisty Celtic warrior queen Boudicca challenged the Roman 9th legion in AD 61.

❶ From the car park, cross a small bridge across a tributary and head south-west across the meadow towards a gate. Go through the gate and then follow the path beside the River Welland. When you reach the stone seat with Boudicca's plaque on it, look back to enjoy the splendid view of Stamford.

❷ From here, continue to follow the path beside the meandering river for a few hundred metres until you reach the metal Broadeng footbridge, which marks the furthest point of the walk.

❸ Setting back towards Stamford, follow the path that bisects the meadow, and at a fork take the left path leading towards a gate. Go through the gate, leaving the meadows.

❹ Once through the gate, follow Melancholy Walk, which begins just in front of you. It is a raised path next to a water channel. To your right are good views across the meadow, while on your left are some of Stamford's well-established allotment gardens. At the end of Melancholy Walk, past a small row of houses on your right, turn left up the hill. When you reach Austin Street, turn right.

❺ Carry on along Austin Street – calling in for refreshments at St Peter's Inn via its back entrance, if you like – until you reach the cobbled King's Mill Lane. Turn right downhill and return to the car park at the start of the walk. Near here is another pub, The George, a famous coaching inn.

access information

Parking is available in the car park at Stamford meadows. There is a regular train service to Stamford station – the start of the walk is two minutes from the station. Go to www.railtrack.co.uk for information on train times.

further information

This is an excellent walk for children as it is easy and not too long – take along some bread to feed the ducks. Look out for the remains of the castle wall at the start of the walk, and for the plaque on a small stone seat beside the river commemorating Queen Boudicca. For further information, go to the Stamford website www.stamford.co.uk.

▲ Map: Explorer 15
▲ Distance: 7 km/4¼ miles
▲ Walk ID: 27 Nicholas Rudd-Jones

Difficulty rating

Time

▲ River, Pub, Church, Birds, Flowers, Great Views

Harringworth Viaduct and Seaton

As you will see on this walk, river valleys are home to some of Britain's prettiest wild flowers.

The Welland Valley is one of the most rewarding places to walk in an otherwise rather flat landscape. The walk first hugs the pretty River Welland, then climbs to the ridge to give fine views of the valley.

❶ At Harringworth, go through the church gates and follow the path on the south side to another gate. Turn right through a riding centre and carry on to the road. Turn left along a path by the side of the road for a short distance.

❷ Follow a footpath to the left, through a gate and immediately over a stile. Head diagonally to the right across the field to the river. Turn right and follow the river to the Turtle Bridge. Turn left over the bridge along a stone track, which soon crosses a disused railway line. Follow the track up the slope to the road.

❸ Turn left and follow the road to the next junction. Turn left again and follow the road to Seaton village. As you come into the village, look for a pub ahead on the right. Turn left just after it in front of the church and head down this road to where a path leads back into the fields. Climb a stile and head diagonally left across the fields towards a railway embankment which rises visibly ahead.

❹ Go up the steps in the embankment – carefully, as they are in poor repair – and go down the other side. Cross the road and follow the footpath down a track leading to a private house. Just before the house, skirt round to the left, then veer right. Cross a little footbridge, then immediately climb a stile on the left. Follow the path diagonally left over the fields.

❺ Head towards the viaduct, which you will pass under. At the end of the field, just beyond the viaduct, there is a gate and a stile. Climb the stile. You are now back in Harringworth village. Turn left and at the White Swan pub turn left again to your car.

further information

For information on the Harringworth viaduct, go to http://www.skynet.co.uk/maurice/northants/nviaduct.htm.
The White Swan pub in Harringworth has good food and welcomes children.

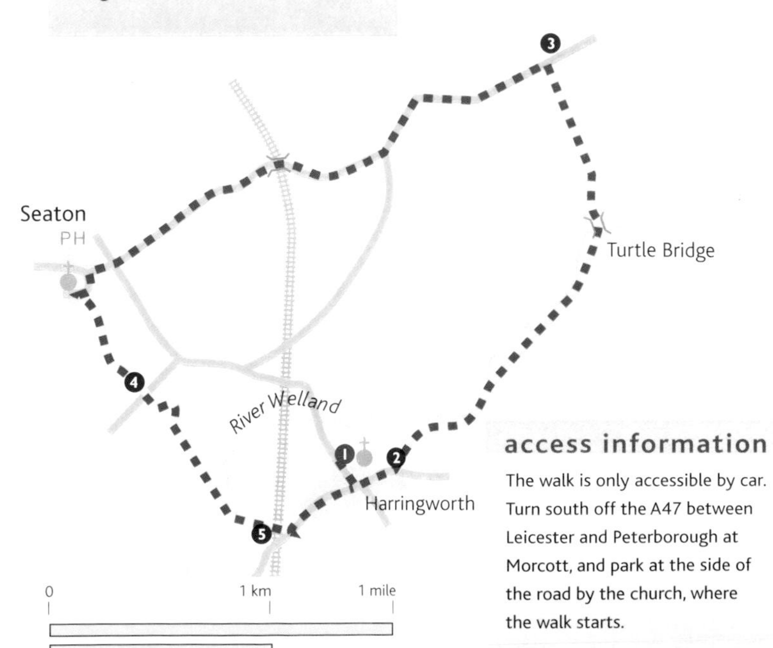

access information

The walk is only accessible by car. Turn south off the A47 between Leicester and Peterborough at Morcott, and park at the side of the road by the church, where the walk starts.

▲ Map: Explorer 207
▲ Distance: 13.69 km/8½ miles
▲ Walk ID: 1301 R. and J. Glynn

Difficulty rating

Time

▲ River, Pub, Church, Wildlife, Birds, Flowers, Great Views, Butterflies, Food Shop

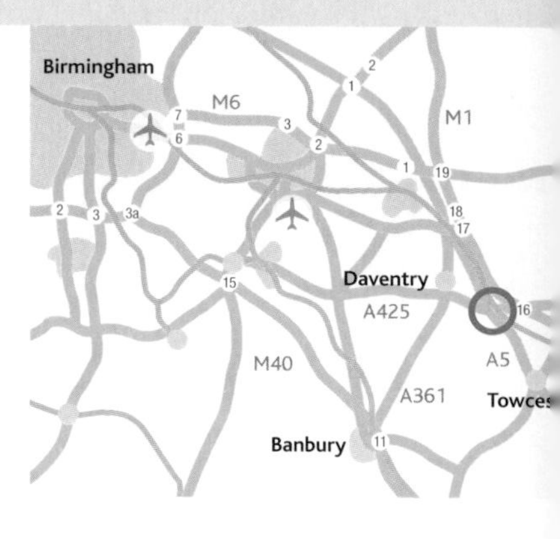

Nether Heyford from Weedon

This diverse walk follows the Nene Way, then the towpath beside the Grand Union Canal, before following footpaths through fields and meadows to the pretty village of Nether Heyford. The route continues through a beautiful rural landscape, passing Bugbrooke Mill and village before rejoining the canal towpath.

❶ From Weedon Post Office, follow the road to the railway bridge. Past St Peter's churchyard, turn right on the Nene Way. Cross the road and carry on. Fork right off the old Wharf House drive. Cross the canal at bridge 25, go down the steps, then turn left along the towpath. Turn left at bridge 27 and left along the road.

❷ Turn right at the footpath, crossing two fields, then a third, bearing slightly right. Cross a footbridge, a stile and more meadows to a footbridge into a field. Cross a hard track and climb the stile to the right, then cross another field. Climb the stile, and follow the path, turning right by a wall into Nether Heyford.

❸ Turn left into Church Lane. Go through the church gate, then turn left. Follow the footpath between trees, then two walls. Cross a narrow road and follow the path opposite. Cross the estate road and carry on. Opposite Brookside Close, turn right.

❹ Turn left on the Kislingbury footpath. Cross the river, then go through the kissing gate on the left and follow the field edge. Turn left through another gate, following the field edge to the right. Go through two more gates. Following the hedge line, enter a small copse. Follow the River Nene for a short distance, then take the hard track away.

❺ Turn right on the footpath across the fields to Bugbrooke. Climb the stile, follow a narrow path to the road and turn right. At the junction, turn right into Church Lane. Passing the church, turn right towards Weedon, then left on the Old Crown footpath.

❻ Turn right at the canal bridge and follow the towpath. Soon after Flore Lane Bridge, climb the stile and follow a track through meadowland. Cross a large field towards a white building. Climb the stile in the corner. Walk up to the road and cross over. Join the Nene Way opposite, and walk along to the canal bridge. Return to the start point.

further information

The walk recalls a time when the Grand Union Canal was an essential route, along which boatmen and their families would travel to and from London with their cargoes. Flour is still produced at Bugbrooke Mill, and in the graveyard of Bugbrooke Church look out for an inscription from Longfellow on a tree.

access information

Weedon lies south of the A5 between Daventry and Northampton. Street parking is available in the village.

The Grand Union Canal, which crosses this route, is a semi-permanent home for houseboat-dwellers.

This walk takes in a beautiful English church.

▲ Map: Explorer 191
▲ Distance: 8.86 km/5½ miles
▲ Walk ID: 858 R. and J. Glynn

Difficulty rating

Time ●●●

▲ Church, Wildlife, Birds, Flowers, Great Views, Butterflies

A422
A43
Banbury
Brackley
A361
A4260
M40
Oxford

Nell Bridge and Kings Sutton from Twyford Wharf

This walk emphasises the peace and tranquillity of the canal environment. Willows droop lazily at the water's edge, and there are lovely renovated cottages and pretty gardens. Look out for the old-fashioned drawbridges, a characteristic of this canal.

❶ From the bridge at Twyford Wharf, go down on to the canal towpath and turn left to walk under the bridge. As you walk, you will see the silhouette of Kings Sutton Church and spire. Continue along the towpath.

❷ At Nell Bridge Lock, leave the canal, turning left by the road bridge to walk alongside the road, crossing the border into Northamptonshire. Turn left to follow a minor road towards Kings Sutton.

❸ Follow the first footpath sign on the left across a field. Go through a gap in the hedge, and cross another field. Climb a stile and head diagonally right, towards an ivy-clad dead tree, where a footbridge crosses a stream. Climb another stile and carry on, towards a weighted wooden gate. Cross a track and go through two more gates.

❹ Carry on, with the lovely setting of the Manor House and Kings Sutton Church on your right. Head towards a kissing gate, hidden under a clump of trees. Do not go through the gate, but turn left to walk beside the stone wall beneath the spreading oaks.

❺ Turn right down a bank on a signed footpath, above the railway station. Walk over rough ground towards the village street. Cross, and follow the footpath

The elegant spire on Kings Sutton Church provides a walker's landmark.

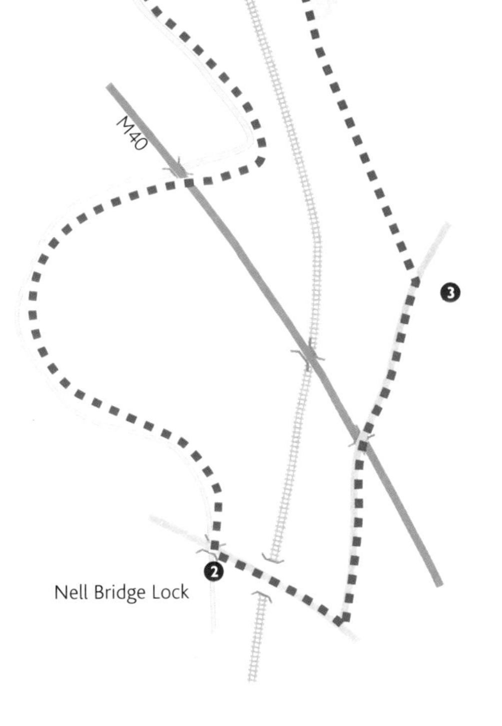

sign opposite, between houses. Go through two more gates, passing an enclosed bog spring on the way. Cross a footbridge and a large meadow. Cross another footbridge and continue in the same direction, gradually nearing the railway embankment.

❻ Turn left to climb a stile, and cross the railway track at the designated place. Go down the embankment, cross another footbridge, then carry on, heading towards the road across another large meadow. The path very gradually leaves the railway line. Turn left over a stile and walk along the road to Twyford Wharf and bridge.

One of the joys of this footpath is the sight of willows lining the water's edge.

access information

From Banbury, turn left off the A4260 towards Kings Sutton. A small lay-by just before the canal bridge is suitable for limited parking.

further information

Be prepared to have your peace shattered for just a little while where the M40 crosses the canal at drawbridge 183. This brief intrusion is more than compensated by the peace to be found on the rest of the walk.

▲ Map: Explorer 180
▲ Distance: 12 km/7½ miles
▲ Walk ID: 269 Oliver O'Brien

Difficulty rating

Time

▲ River, Pub, Canal, Toilets, Museum, Church, Wildlife, Birds, Flowers, Great Views

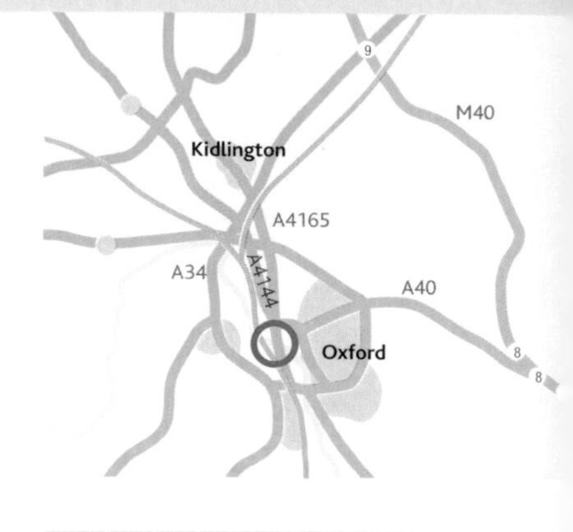

Oxford, Godstow and Port Meadow

From the heart of Oxford, this is a complete circuit of Port Meadow. The first half follows the Thames Path National Trail to Godstow, with its lock, ruined abbey and famous Trout Inn. The return walk follows the Oxford Canal back to the city centre.

❶ From the traffic lights by Folly Bridge, follow the Thames Path west, passing a barrier and crossing a small bridge. Pass an old crane and bear right where the path meets the road, staying by the Thames bank. Cross under a bridge and continue along the path right on the river bank.

❷ Immediately after the railway bridges, cross a bridge over a tributary and continue alongside the main river. Pass through Osney Lock and carry on. Bear left slightly and cross a footbridge. Crossing the road with care, cross the bridge on the pavement. On the other side, continue along the signposted Thames Path.

❸ At the next bridge, take the signposted path to the left, following the Thames. Cross a bright red bridge over the river and carry on, passing a boatyard to the left. Pass through a small gate and continue on the Thames Path.

❹ Pass Godstow Lock and the abbey ruins. Bear slightly right off the main path up to the road. Go through the gate, and turn right over the narrow bridge. Follow the road through Wolvercote. Crossing the big road bridge, follow a path down about halfway along on the left, and bear right. Pass Wolvercote Lock and under the bridges, then follow the towpath.

❺ Cross the black-and-white bridge on to an 'island'. Continue along the path. When the canal ends, cross the busy road, turn right and cross a bridge. Immediately, follow a path signposted 'Mill Stream Walk', which crosses another busy road. The path eventually turns into a road which bears round to the left. Turn left at the next junction.

❻ Turn right and walk along Queen Street to Carfax. Turn right and walk right down St Aldates. Continue down the road, passing two sets of traffic lights, and cross Folly Bridge to the start of the walk.

access information

Oxford's bus and train stations are both in the city centre, so are near the start and finish of the walk.

Oxford is difficult to get around by car, and parking is extremely difficult. Either park in a suburb of Oxford and walk in, or use the park-and-ride service.

In time-honoured tradition, rowers make their regular progress along the River Cherwell at Oxford.

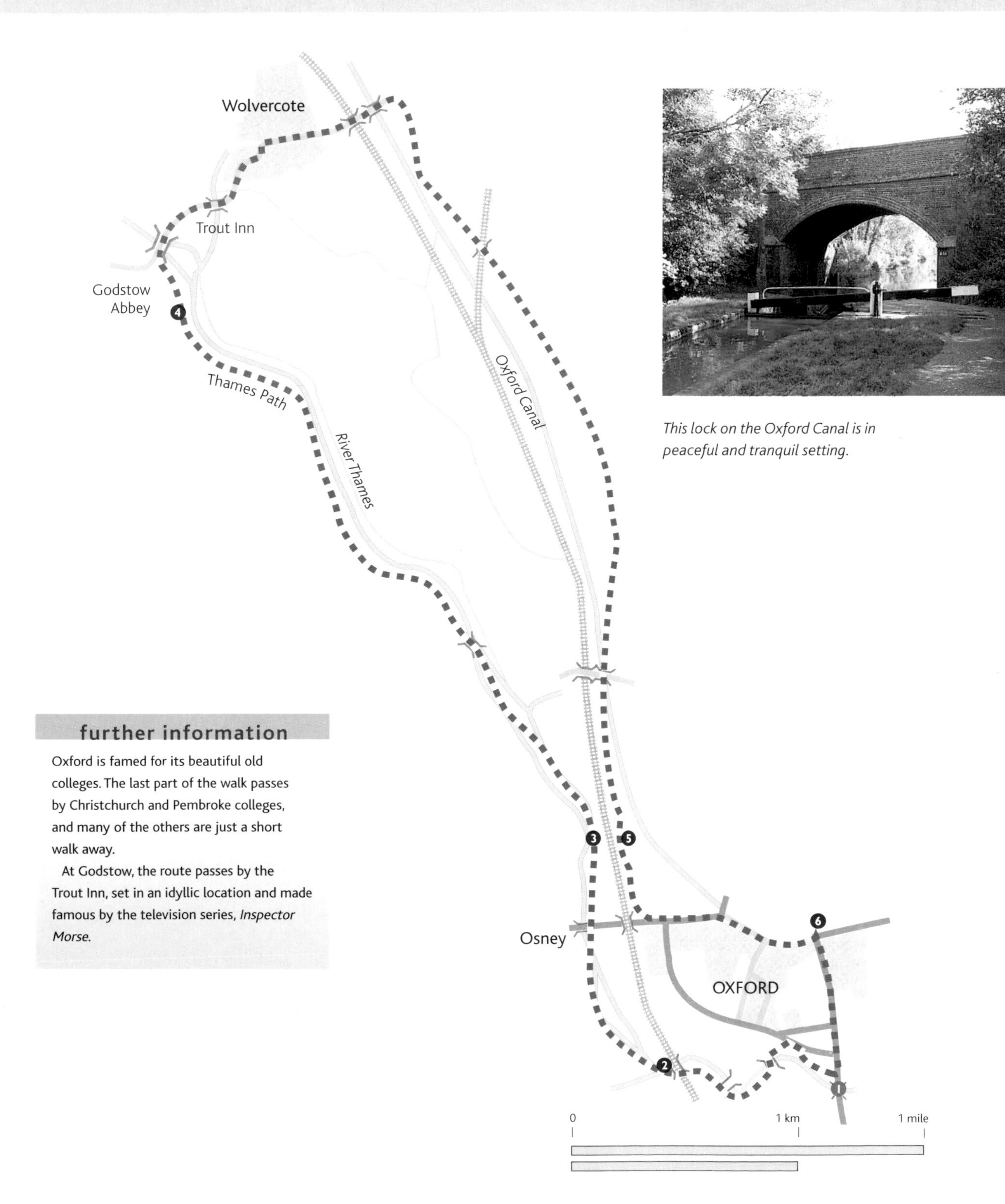

This lock on the Oxford Canal is in peaceful and tranquil setting.

further information

Oxford is famed for its beautiful old colleges. The last part of the walk passes by Christchurch and Pembroke colleges, and many of the others are just a short walk away.

At Godstow, the route passes by the Trout Inn, set in an idyllic location and made famous by the television series, *Inspector Morse*.

▲ Map: Explorer 191
▲ Distance: 12.88 km/8 miles
▲ Walk ID: 367 R. and J. Glynn

Difficulty rating

Time

▲ River, Pub, Church, Birds, Great Views

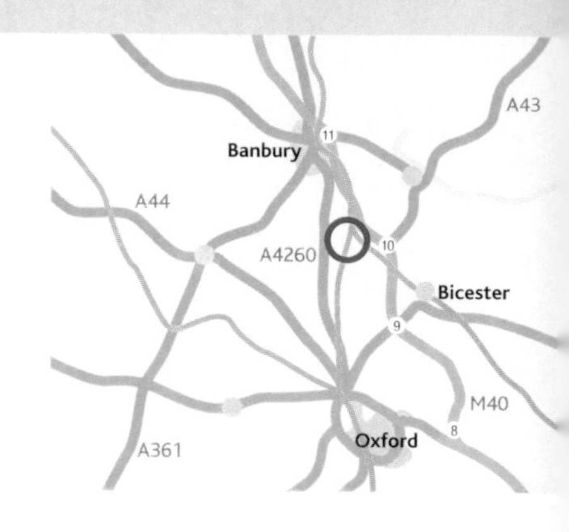

The Heyfords from Somerton

Starting from the beautiful village of Somerton, this walk gives fine views across the Cherwell Valley. The Heyfords are charming and interesting villages alongside the Southern Oxford Canal.

❶ Cross the canal bridge and walk under the railway bridge and uphill into the village of Somerton. When you reach the junction with the Ardley road at Yew Tree Cottage, turn left and follow the road for some distance.

❷ Turn right on to a bridleway leading to Upper Heyford. Walk past a farm, bearing left to follow the track in the same direction, then walk along the perimeter fence of the now disused Heyford Airbase. Continue to follow the fence as the path turns right and then left.

❸ Turn right across a field, heading for a gap, and come out on the road. Turn left towards the houses, passing the Barley Mow pub on your left. Turn right into the High Street and walk through the village of Upper Heyford. Take the left fork into School Lane and walk along to the church.

❹ Take the path on the left, through a kissing gate and across the meadow to another gate. Turn left, then right along a hard track, through a gate and along to the sewage works. Climb a stile on the left and walk with the hedge on your right. Follow the fence when it turns right, then turn left away from it along the edge of the field. Follow this path, with the canal on your right, to Lower Heyford village hall.

❺ Turn right on to the road to cross the drawbridge, then turn right on to the canal towpath. You now have the canal on your right and the River Cherwell on your left. Continue the walk back along the towpath, through the flood meadows, and leave the path at bridge 96 to return to the start of the walk.

further information

The flood meadows of the River Cherwell run alongside the towpath of part of the Southern Oxford Canal, and when flooded can look like a vast lake. Locks and graceful arched bridges add charm and interest as the walk meanders back along the canal.

This bank along the route of the River Cherwell is the perfect picnic place.

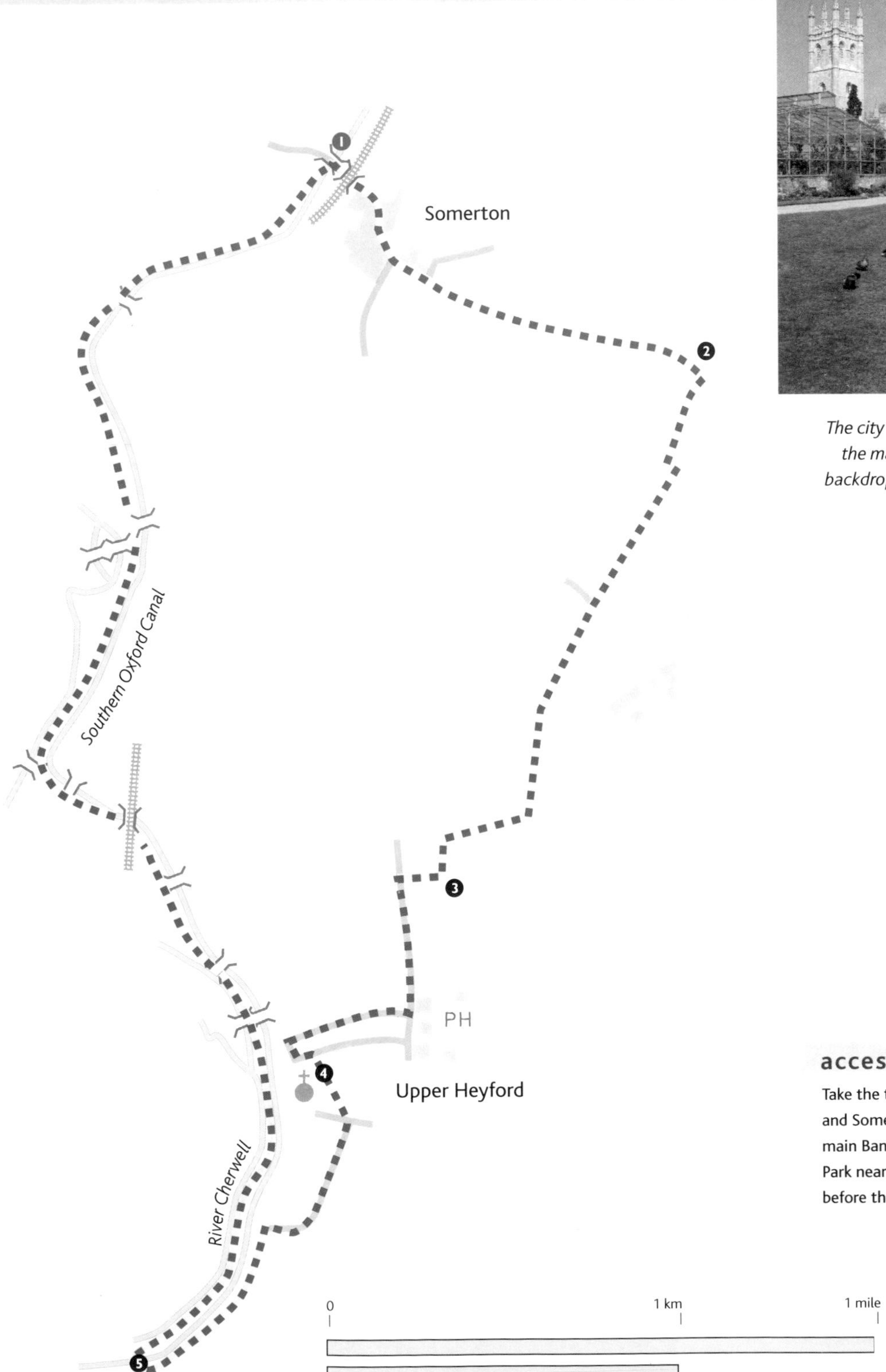

The city of Oxford provides the magnificent urban backdrop for the Cherwell.

access information

Take the turning to North Aston and Somerton off the A4260 main Banbury to Oxford road. Park near the canal bridge just before the village of Somerton.

▲ Map: Explorer 222
▲ Distance: 9.66 km/6 miles
▲ Walk ID: 1481 R. and J. Glynn

Difficulty rating

Time

▲ Lake, Pub, Church, Wildlife, Birds, Flowers, Great Views, Butterflies, Food Shop

Calcutt Locks from Stockton

This great little walk can almost be entitled 'a marina walk', as it visits three – Ventnor Farm Marina and Calcutt Marina, both on the Grand Union Canal, and Napton Marina, on the North Oxford Canal.

❶ Following the Napton road, cross the sports field to a gap in the far corner. Follow the field edge to the stile. Turn left on the road. At the metal gate, turn right and cross a field diagonally left, then a large meadow, following the hedge. Cross another meadow, then climb two stiles through pasture, heading for the top left corner.

❷ Turn left on a track, then right at the road. Turn left through the gate opposite Hill Cottage on to a bridleway. Go through another gate and follow the path. Turn left over Tomlow Bridge, left on to the towpath, and left again under the bridge to walk beside the Grand Union Canal.

❸ At Calcutt Locks, walk to the top of the flight. Cross the top lock gate, then a footbridge by the shop, turning left by the railings. Turn right over the footbridge, then left. Turn right through an opening between the two sections of reservoir. Crossing a wooden bridge, turn left.

❹ Turn right through a signed gap in the fence and cross the meadow to a gap in the hedge. Cross another meadow. Enter another field, aiming for a stile at the top. Walk over to a metal gate and on to the North Oxford Canal towpath. Turn right under the bridge and walk to bridge 111. Turn right through a gate to the road.

❺ Turn immediately right through a gate and cross two fields. Cross a stile, a footbridge, and three more fields. Climb the stile and follow the edge of two more fields. When the hedge turns away, walk on, cross a stile and a footbridge, and head towards the sewage works. Cross the next field to the stile in the corner. Turn left on to a track, then right on a private road. Follow the road back into Stockton.

Taking a barge down the Grand Union Canal.

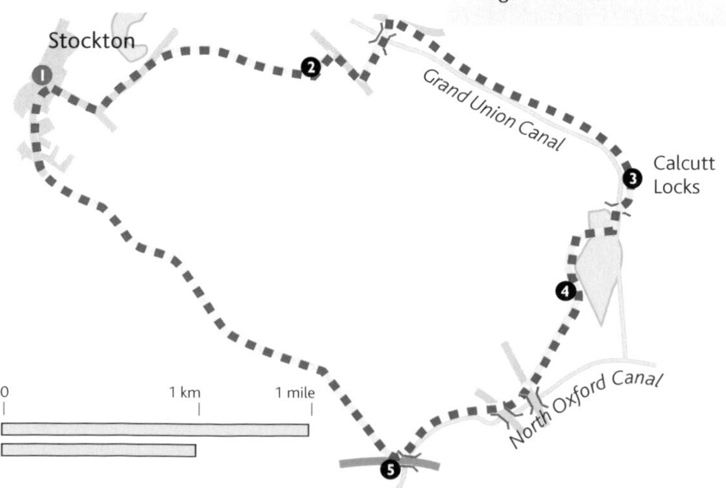

further information

The paths across the fields and meadows are well-defined and easy to follow. The Napton Reservoir is surrounded by natural meadowland, where wonderful wild flowers grow. There is also a huge reed bed near the point at which you head away from the reservoir. As you walk, look out for the Napton Windmill – it comes into view near the start of the route, and again at the reservoir.

access information

From the A423 Banbury to Coventry road, take the A426 towards Rugby, and turn off on an unclassified road to the village of Stockton.

▲ Map: Explorer 221

▲ Distance: 8.86 km/5½ miles

▲ Walk ID: 992 Ron and Jenny Glynn

Difficulty rating

Time

▲ Pub, Stately Home, Birds, Flowers, Great Views, Butterflies, Food Shop, Woodland

The locks at Stratford-upon-Avon.

Saltisford Basin and Hatton Locks

Much of this walk is on the Grand Union Canal towpath, following the dramatic climb of the 21 Hatton Locks. The walk then follows a fine bridleway through very pleasant flat farmland, before rejoining the canal to return to Saltisford Basin.

❶ From the car park, turn right, go through the metal gates, then turn left at the end of Budbrooke Road to walk over the canal bridge. Turn left on the footpath opposite the cemetery. After a short distance, veer left off the footpath and go through a gap down on to the canal towpath. Turn right and walk along the path, passing the first of the 21 Hatton Locks at Hatton Bottom, and then 'Ugly Bridge'.

❷ At bridge 54, the route leaves the canal. Walk with the large white house on your right, and go through the kissing gate in the corner, beneath a tree. Walk uphill to pass the Waterman pub, turning right beside it. Turn right on to the pavement along the road, then cross the road to take the left fork to Beausale.

❸ After a short distance, turn left on to a minor road, which gradually climbs to reach Ashwood Lodge. Turn right on a bridleway towards Turkey Farm House. Go through the metal gate beside the farmhouse and carry on, passing a pond. Turn right at a marker and walk around the field edge.

❹ Go through a gap on the left, beside an oak tree, and follow the edge of the field on a permissive path to the far corner, turning right into the next field. Walk on with Blackbrake Plantation on the left and a wooded area on the right, still following the field edges, which zigzag before Wedgnock Farm. Pass the farm on a track to the right and follow the track to the road. Cross by the traffic lights, and walk along Budbrooke Road ahead, passing the Fire Safety Headquarters before reaching the canal bridge.

❺ Turn right over the road and then go down on to the canal footpath and turn left. Retrace your steps to the Saltisford Basin car park.

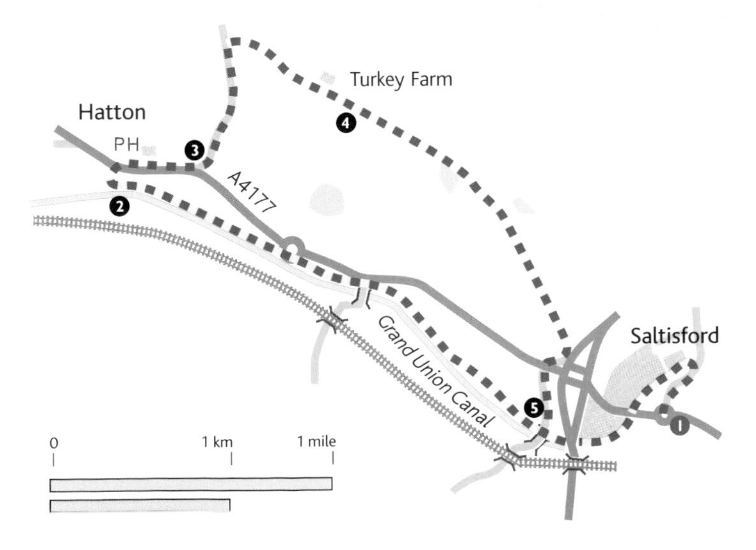

further information

The 21 Hatton Locks are a spectacular sight, with their tall, white-topped paddles, white-tipped gates and white edging around the lock entrances. Once a hubbub of working narrow boats, the locks are now used only by leisure craft, and the sight of a loaded pair of boats, crewed by the boatman and his family, has gone forever.

access information

From the A452 between Warwick and Birmingham, follow the sign to Canal Centre, Saltisford, and turn left into the centre car park.

▲ Map: Explorer 14
▲ Distance: 11.27 km/7 miles
▲ Walk ID: 974 Pat Roberts

Difficulty rating

Time

▲ Hills, Pub, Toilets, National Trust/NTS, Wildlife, Birds, Great Views, Butterflies, Gift Shop, Nature Trail, Tea Shop, Woodland

Herefordshire Beacon and Midsummer Hill from Hollybush NT

This is an energetic but historically interesting walk, taking in two Iron Age hill forts – the British Camp on the Herefordshire Beacon, and Midsummer Hill – as well as the intriguing Giant's Cave. The route is in an area of Special Scientific Interest.

❶ From the car park entrance, follow the signposted Worcestershire Way, which turns from a metalled road to a rougher track as it goes uphill. Carry on until you reach a fingerpost and a kissing gate.

❷ Go through the gate and take the path second from the left to the Obelisk. Return to the Worcestershire Way and continue to follow the path north. At the top of a hill where the ruts in the path become deeper, climb a stile on the right.

❸ Follow the path through the wood to the road at the bottom. Turn left, and after a short distance cross the road to follow the Worcestershire Way markers past a house to a wood. Where the drive bears right, take the path through the wood. Climb a stile into open ground and reach another three-fingered post.

❹ Turn right, signed 'British Camp Car Park' and follow the path through the trees. Cross the A449, and take the hard path to the right of the car park. Zigzag up the hill, following the signs for the British Camp to the top.

❺ Head south along the ridge to a steep stone path, and go down carefully, heading for a marker in the dip. At the marker, take the path to the right signposted 'Giant's Cave'. At the cave, carry on to a T-junction. Take the right-hand path on to Swinyard Hill and follow the ridge until it starts to drop.

❻ Follow the right-hand path, signposted 'Obelisk' and 'Midsummer Hill', to the Worcestershire Way. Turn left, and at the fingerpost and kissing gate follow Worcestershire Way South. Take a path on the left to climb to the top of Midsummer Hill. Head south, gradually losing height, and drop down through a wood to the open ground above the car park.

access information

Hollybush is on the A438 south of Great Malvern. There is a private car park just outside Hollybush belonging to the Eastnor Castle Company. Most of the paths belong to the estate but the public may use the facilities with certain restrictions on cars and bikes. There is a bus service.

The Malvern Hills provide the stunning setting for this energetic walk.

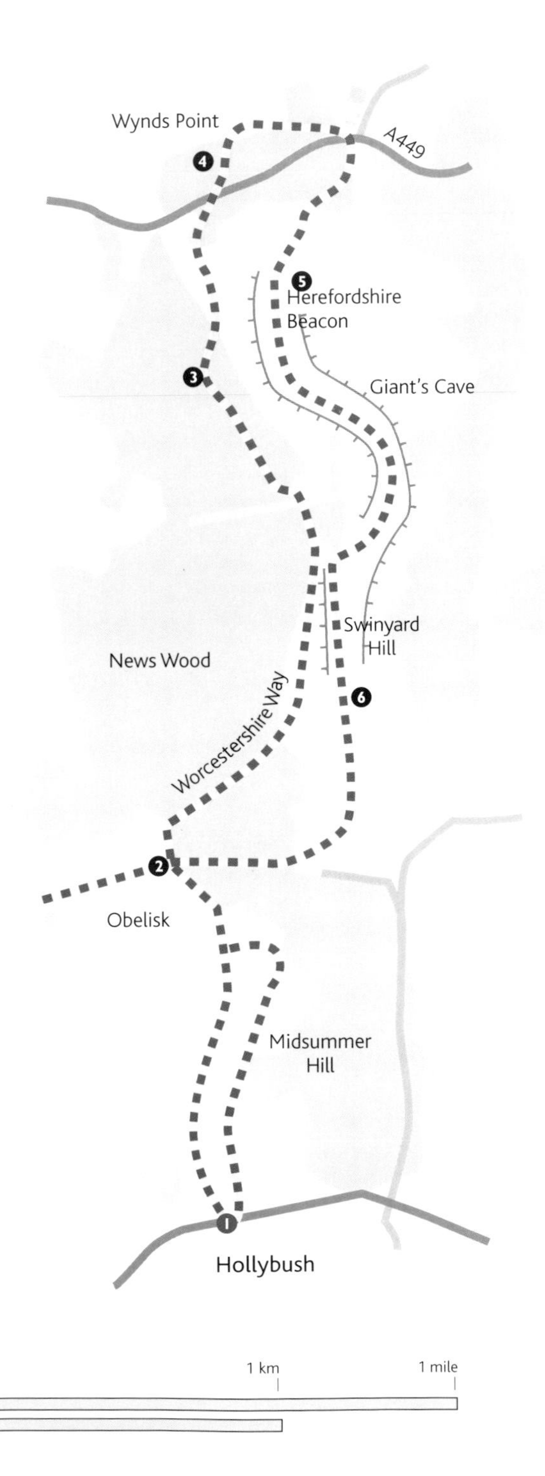

The stark outline of the 11th-century Herefordshire Beacon is a landmark on this walk.

further information

The outward leg of the route includes a detour to see an Obelisk, but as the detour returns to the same point, this can be omitted if time is limited. The walk also passes the Giant's Cave. Although the origins of the cave are unknown, legend has linked it with John Oldcastle and Owen Glendower, or it may have been occupied by a hermit.

▲ Map: Explorer 15
▲ Distance: 6 km/3¾ miles
▲ Walk ID: 32 Nicholas Rudd-Jones

Difficulty rating

Time

▲ Pub, Church, Wildlife, Birds, Flowers

Barnack Hills and Holes

This simple stroll starts at the enchanting and aptly named Barnack Hills and Holes, where ragstone was quarried to build Peterborough Cathedral in the 12th century – you will see a few lumps in the road at Southorpe village.

❶ Choose one of the many paths across the nature reserve and head for the south-west edge. Go through a wooden gate alongside the big stone wall of Walcot Hall.

❷ Follow the path between the wall and a field. At the end of the wall, where the path meets the road, turn left on to a gravelled track marked 'Public Bridleway', passing Walcot Hall on your left. At the next corner of the park wall, continue ahead on another gravelled track.

❸ When the track veers left, keep straight on to the right of a low stone wall ahead of you and take the path along the field edge. Pass through a wooden gate and follow the field edge, heading for a metal gate to the right of two oak trees.

❹ Go through the gate and head for the road, keeping the wall on your right. Turn left on to the road to Southorpe. Where the road starts to veer right at the end of the village, by Hall Farm, climb a stile into a field. Head for a gate and another stile at the far side of the field, then aim for a small group of cottages.

❺ At the cottages, cross the road and go through a wooden gate into fields. Walk towards the left-hand corner of the thin hedge ahead of you. Keep the hedge on your right and follow the path into Barnack village, past the bowling green and cricket ground on your left, alongside a stone wall, and then between trees. At the road, turn left. Follow the road round to the right at the Fox and Hounds pub and take the next left. Shortly afterwards, turn left again, passing the Millstone pub on the way back to the car.

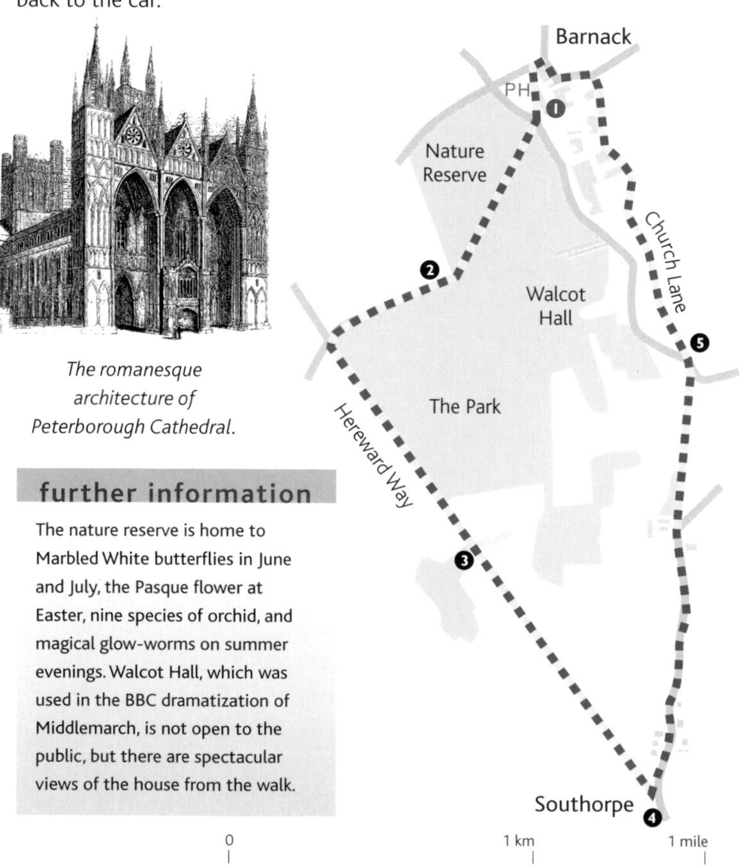

The romanesque architecture of Peterborough Cathedral.

further information

The nature reserve is home to Marbled White butterflies in June and July, the Pasque flower at Easter, nine species of orchid, and magical glow-worms on summer evenings. Walcot Hall, which was used in the BBC dramatization of Middlemarch, is not open to the public, but there are spectacular views of the house from the walk.

access information

Barnack is south of the A16 from Stamford to Market Deeping. Park in a little lay-by at the main entrance to the nature reserve.

▲ Map: Explorer 245
▲ Distance: 4.8 km/3 miles
▲ Walk ID: 920 Jude Howat

Difficulty rating

Time

▲ Lake, Pub, Toilets, Museum, Church, Stately Home, Gift Shop, Food Shop, Good for Kids, Public Transport, Restaurant, Woodland

Woodland in Melbourne Parks.

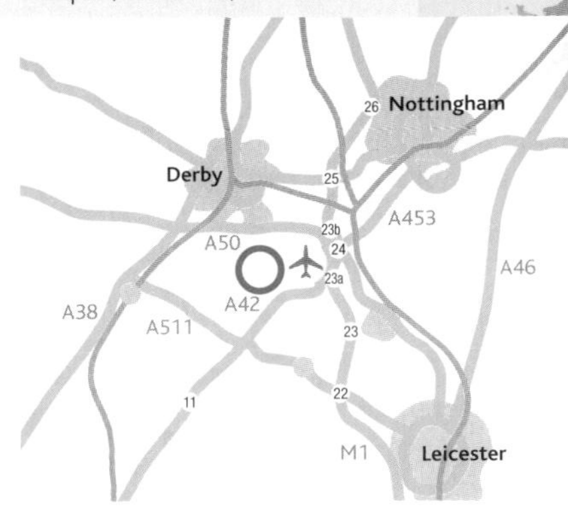

Melbourne Parks

This simple countryside walk begins and ends in the ancient village of Melbourne. The parish church is one of the finest surviving examples of Norman ecclesiastical architecture in the country, and dates from the mid-12th century.

❶ Starting at the junction into Melbourne Hall and park, follow Blackwell Lane out of Melbourne. Just before the road bends to the right, there is a footpath sign on the right. Follow the footpath into the fields. Almost immediately bear half left to a stile and follow the path diagonally across the fields. The next stile is under the trees. Continue across the fields to the main track from the park.

❷ Cross the cattle grid and then a stile, just off to the left. Follow the path diagonally across two fields up the hill towards a big tree and a farmhouse on the horizon. Leave the fields and go through a gap in the trees ahead of you. Follow the path through the next field, going down to join Green Lane.

❸ Turn right and follow the lane until it bends sharply right. Branch left to follow the bridleway. Cross a small stream and carry on. Turn right where the path splits, and head up the hill towards the trees. Follow the path through the woods and come out in a small field.

❹ Cross the field to another plantation of trees, called Paddock Pool. Cross a small bridge over a stream and come out of the woods into another field. Cross the field to its far diagonal corner. Turn right and cross the stile. The path continues along a grassy lane.

❺ As the lane bends left to the farmhouse, keep right and aim for the trees ahead. Climb a few steps to a stile, then continue on the right-hand edge of the next field. Follow the footpath signs through the fields.

❻ Leaving the last field, join the metalled track through Melbourne Park. Turn left and walk towards the Melbourne Pool. Following this track, return to the start of the walk.

access information

Melbourne is off the A514 south of Derby. Pass through Stanton-by-Bridge and take the B587 towards Melbourne. In Melbourne, follow signs for Melbourne Hall. There is limited parking outside the church.

further information

Melbourne is the second largest town in South Derbyshire, with a population of around 5,000. This ancient town is in the centre of a fertile market gardening area.

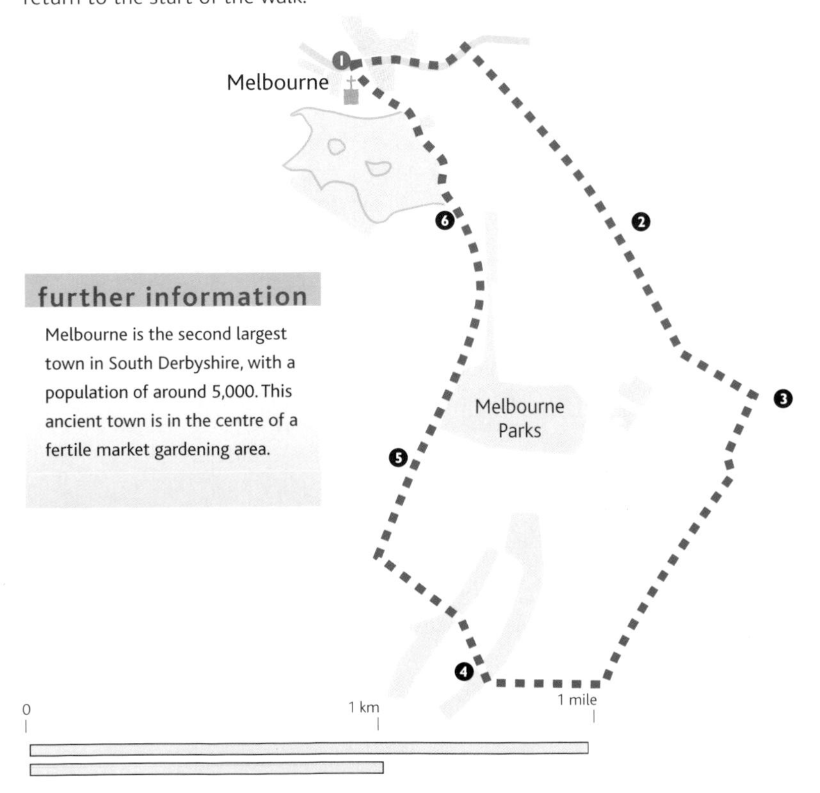

▲ Map: Explorer 24
▲ Distance: 10 km/6¼ miles
▲ Walk ID: 1545 Jim Grindle

Difficulty rating

Time

▲ Hills or Fells, Pubs, Toilets, Church, National Trust/NTS, Wildlife, Flowers, Great Views, Butterflies, Good for Kids, Public Transport, Woodland, Ancient Monument

The Nine Ladies and Robin Hood's Stride from Winster

This wonderfully varied walk takes you up hill and down dale, although not too steeply. Along the way, there is a prehistoric stone circle known as the Nine Ladies. There are rocks to climb up and through, and pleasant views of the Peak District.

❶ From the junction near the car park, take the right-hand road to the village. Walk up the lane opposite the Market House and a little to the left. Climb a stile into a field on the left. Follow the left-hand flagged path to a fence with two stiles.

❷ Climb the right-hand stile and follow the path uphill and through the trees. Cross over the next track, through the gate and up the hill. Where four paths meet, go straight on past the barn and follow the field edge to the lane. Climb the stile, turn right, and climb another stile on the left.

❸ Fork right towards a rock tower. At the next stile, turn left, following the fence to a tower. Passing the tower, climb a stile on the left and walk to the stone circle. Turn left and follow a broad track to a crossing track by a hut circle. Turn right, walk to the lane and turn left.

❹ Walk across the car park opposite the quarry buildings. Go between two sculptures to follow the path beyond through the trees to Birchover. Turn right along a No Through Road. Follow the stony track at the end, going straight on at the next two crossing tracks.

❺ Climb the stile and head left over the field to another stile. Turn left and at a junction with a narrow lane turn right up a gravelled farm track. At a gap in a wall, follow the left field-edge. Go through a gate and follow the fence on your left. Climb the stile to Robin Hood's Stride.

❻ Retrace your steps and follow the narrow lane. At the junction, cross over and follow the gravelled track to the next road junction. Turn left and head for the next junction. Cross the green strip and follow the lane opposite to the car park.

access information

Winster is 4 miles west of Matlock on the B5057. The no 172 bus runs from Matlock to the village.

The gently undulating path takes the walker past the prehistoric stone circles known as the Nine Ladies.

further information

The climb on to Stanton Moor is well worthwhile as the walk around its edge gives good views of the woodland and valley below. You can also see tree houses that were built and inhabited by protesters against a quarry extension. The efforts of earlier protesters are commemorated by a tower built to mark the passing of the 19th-century Reform Act.

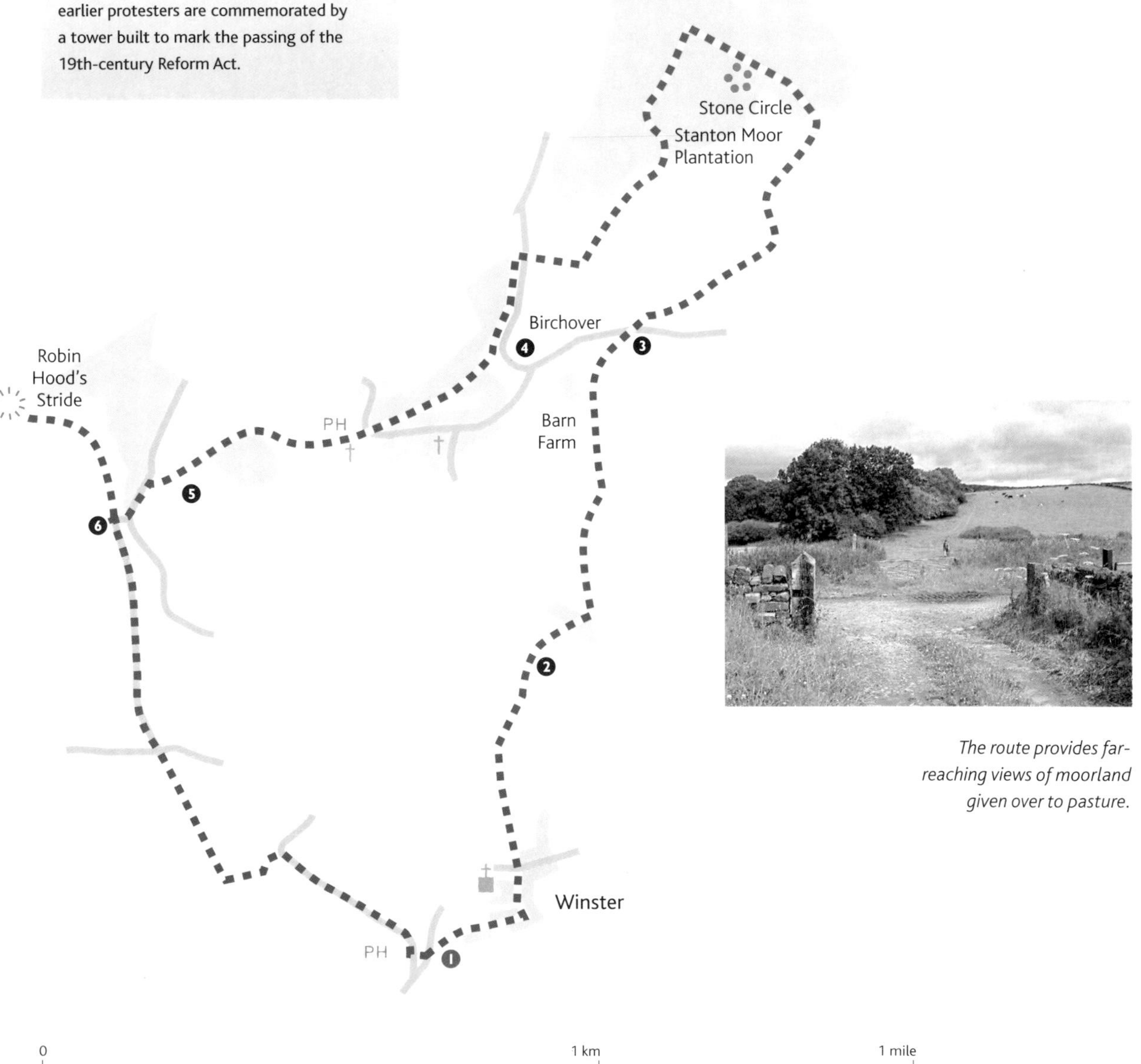

The route provides far-reaching views of moorland given over to pasture.

▲ Map: Explorer 15
▲ Distance: 8 km/5 miles
▲ Walk ID: 9 Nicholas Rudd-Jones

Difficulty rating

Time

▲ River, Pub, Toilets, Museum, Church, Wildlife, Birds, Flowers, Great Views

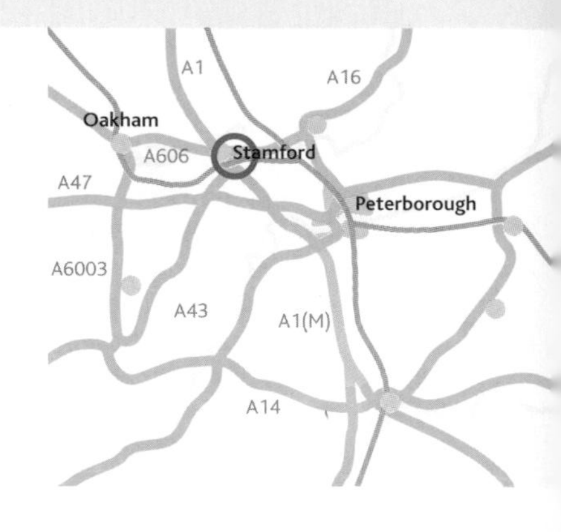

Easton on the Hill from Stamford

This splendid walk begins in Stamford Meadows and carries on to give fine views of the Welland Valley. The route passes through Easton, a typical Welland Valley village, and returns to Stamford through glorious countryside and woodland.

❶ From the car park, cross a bridge across a tributary and cross the meadow to a gate. Go through and follow the path across the meadow. Pass the stone seat with a plaque commemorating Queen Boudicca, and follow the river to the Broadeng Bridge. Cross over and continue to follow the river.

❷ Follow a marked path slightly to the left and go through the tunnel under the A1. Cross a bridge and a field, and climb the wooden steps up and over the railway crossing. On the other side, walk through an overgrown stretch into a long field. Follow the path leading up towards the Easton slope.

❸ At the corner of the field, go through a gap in the hedge and cross the field to a stile. Climb this stile and the next one and carry on to Easton, coming out in Church Street. Turn left at the church into the village. After the War Memorial, turn left to the A43 and turn left again for a short distance. Cross carefully to a signed footpath.

❹ Follow this track, passing first between two fields and then through the woods. With the Wothorpe ruins on your right, walk down a stone track then climb a stile to a footpath on your right. Walk down towards the A1.

❺ Go through the tunnel under the A1 and immediately turn right, following the field edge to the next field. Turn left towards Stamford. Climb a stile, cross the field and climb another stile.

❻ Follow the path between houses then walk along an entrance road. The path continues between two hedges to the left of a Victorian house. At the next field, cross diagonally left to a bridge over a stream. Cross another field to the main road. Cross straight over and walk back to the meadows.

The resident deer at Stamford Meadows are just a small part of the wildlife interest in this area.

further information

There are many types of butterflies to be seen in the woods on this walk, particularly Peacocks, Red Admirals, Small Tortoiseshells and Speckled Woods. A good time to see butterflies is late September when the ivy comes into flower, a valuable source of nectar for the long winter months ahead.

access information

Parking is available in the car park at Stamford meadows.

There is a regular train service to Stamford station – the start of the walk is two minutes from the station. Go to www.railtrack.co.uk for information on train times.

The Peacock (far left) and the Red Admiral (left) are just two of the many types of butterfly that can be found in the woods along this walk.

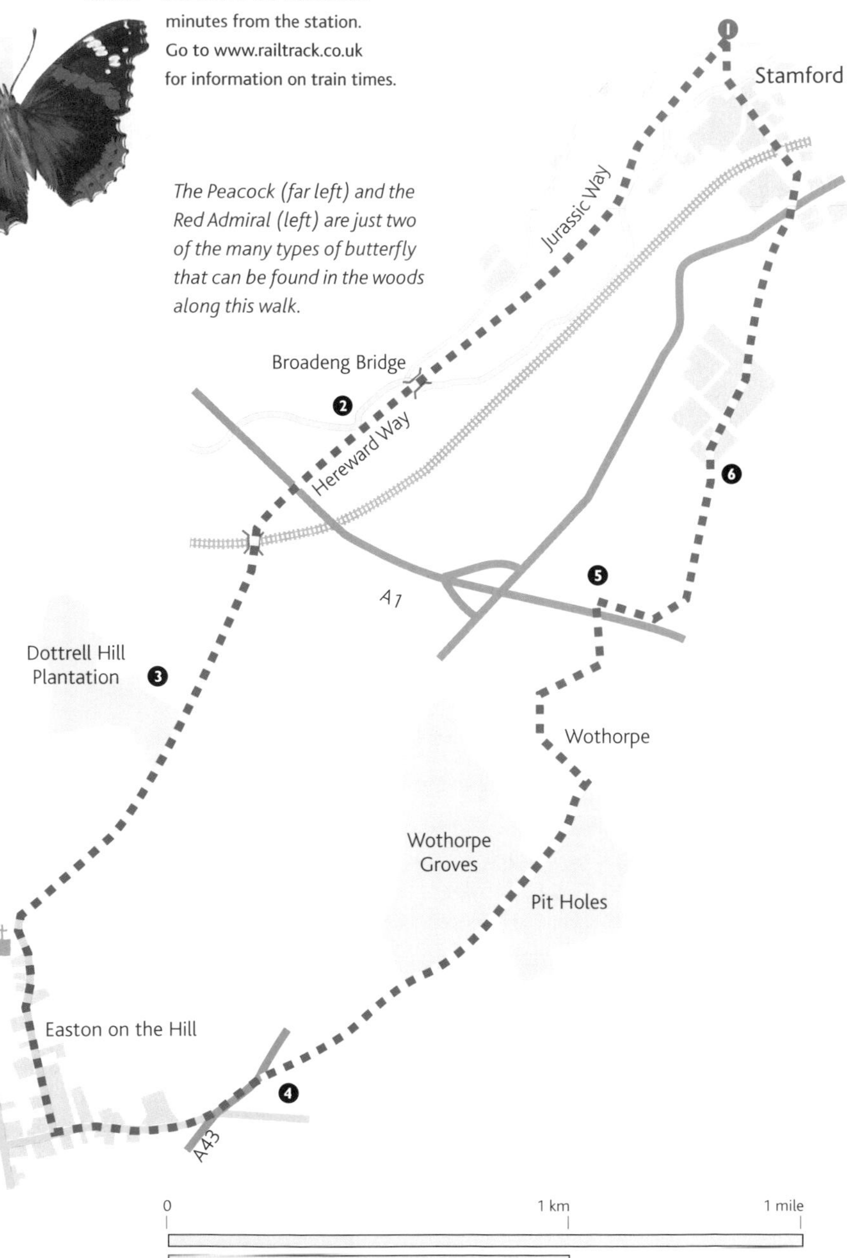

▲ Map: Explorer 273
▲ Distance: 13.69 km/8½ miles
▲ Walk ID: 473 E. Hutchinson

Difficulty rating

Time

▲ Hills, Pub, Churches, Wildlife, Birds, Flowers, Great Views

Tetford and Worlaby from Maidenwell

This walk in the Lincolnshire Wolds descends to Farforth and follows a wonderful deserted valley to Oxcombe. From Tetford there is a steep climb, skirting Worlaby to Ruckland. If time permits, visit the churches at Oxcombe, Tetford and Ruckland.

❶ From the starting point, go through the gate and walk diagonally left across the field towards some trees. The path joins a track which leads to a metal footpath sign. Turn right, keeping the hedge on your left. Follow the path, descending first to pass a wood then following the valley to Oxcombe. If you wish, make a detour to the church.

❷ Turn right and walk along the lane to the first waymark on the left. Cross a small paddock to another lane and turn left. At the next junction, turn right towards Belchford, then turn left on the bridleway towards Glebe Farm Low Yard. After a short distance turn left at another waymark and follow the bridleway to Tetford.

❸ At Tetford, go straight ahead and bear left at the first junction. Visit the church if you like, then follow the lane to the left of the church. At the end go through the cottage entrance. Cross a stile left of the greenhouse. Follow the path across a small paddock, over a stile and up and over the hill. Follow the path through a paddock.

❹ Climb another stile and turn left on the track, then diagonally right across the field. Turn right and cross the road. Beside the gate to Worlaby Farm, cross the stile, the paddock and another stile to follow the well-waymarked farm road through the estate grounds.

❺ At the end of the estate road, turn right. Detour to Ruckland Church if you wish. The walk route turns left at the top of a bank. Follow the path, which is clearly waymarked all the way to Farforth. At Farforth, turn right on to the lane and then left by some fencing. Follow the track ahead to rejoin the track you started out on.

access information

Farforth lies west of the A16 Louth to Skegness road. A wide verge provides good parking for an unlimited number of cars.

The soft curves of the Lincolnshire Wolds provide captivating views.

This typical Lincolnshire churchyard, complete with tiny church, is one of several peaceful spots that may be encountered along this route.

further information

Parts of the walk are extremely exposed to the elements, so dress appropriately. The contributor of this walk offers holiday cottage/guest-house accommodation and logistical support for long-distance walkers at Manor House Swaby. Contact echutchinson@ntlworld.com

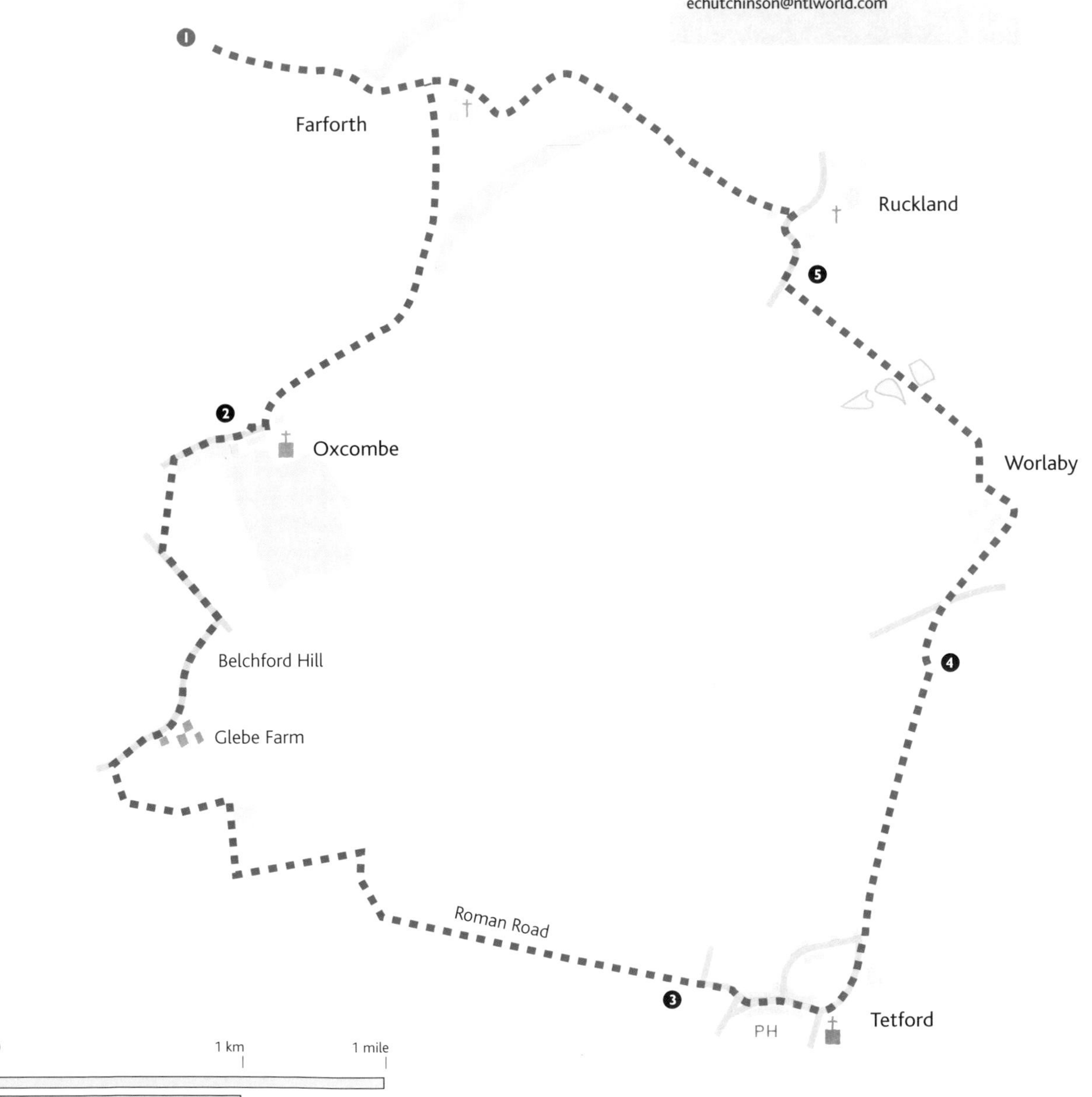

▲ Map: Explorer 238
▲ Distance: 4.83 km/3 miles
▲ Walk ID: 1504 J. and C. Boldero

Difficulty rating

Time

▲ Church, Stately Home, Wildlife, Birds, Flowers, Great Views, Butterflies

Alderford Common

This short and unchallenging countryside walk is not far from Norwich. The route passes through woodland and along tracks, across meadows and through the rural village of Swannington.

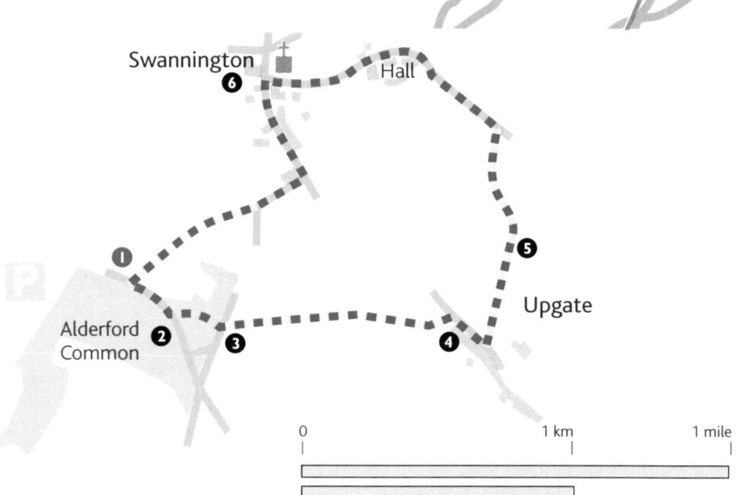

❶ From the Alderford Common car park, turn right along the road.

❷ Turn left at a fingerpost sign on to a woodland path, which goes first through bracken then through open spaces. Follow the path to the top of a bank, then follow it up and down until it goes up some steps.

❸ Turn left along the road, then almost immediately turn right along a track at a fingerpost. Follow the track straight ahead until it reaches a country lane.

❹ Turn right along the lane. Opposite the footpath in Upgate, turn left across the grass to a yellow marker in the far hedgeline. Cross a plank bridge, go up the bank and continue along the field edge.

❺ Turn right at the yellow marker signs, over a bridge and through a gate. Turn left along the meadow, go through the gate, and cross diagonally right under the wires to the next gate. Cross the next meadow to the gate ahead. Turn left and follow the tarmac lane past Swannington Hall.

❻ At the church, turn left along the lane. Follow The Street through Swannington, then bear right along Broad Lane. At the bend, turn right at the fingerpost along a track. Turn left through the hedge at the footpath marker on the ground and follow the path across two fields. Cross the road back to the car park.

The formal gardens of the the moated Tudor manor house, Swannington Hall, contain some fine examples of topiary.

access information

The car park is on Alderford Common, which is on the Reepham to Hellesdon road, 4.8 km south-east of Reepham.

further information

Alderford Common is a designated Site of Special Scientific Interest and is said to be a haven for wildlife. The National Nightingale Survey of 1988 recorded more pairs of nightingales here than anywhere else in east Norfolk. On the south side of the common is an overgrown Bronze Age barrow.

▲ Map: Explorer OL 40
▲ Distance: 8.86 km/5½ miles
▲ Walk ID: 1177 J. and C. Boldero

Difficulty rating

Time

▲ Pub, Toilets, Church, Wildlife, Birds, Flowers, Great Views, Butterflies, Food Shop

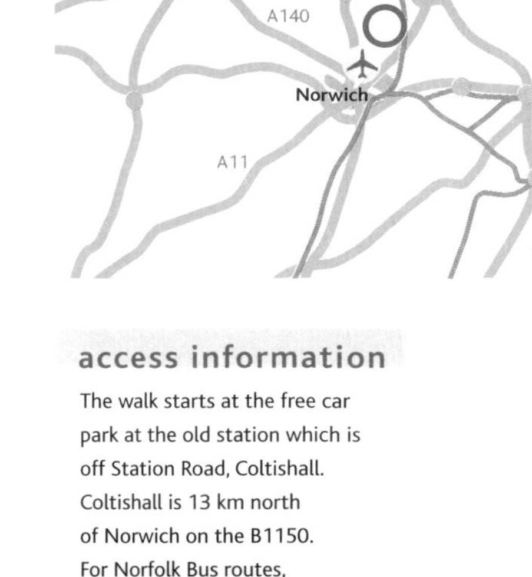

Belaugh from Coltishall

This walk follows the old railway line, following alongside the Bure Valley Railway narrow gauge track, which operates services in summer from Aylsham to Wroxham, then along footpaths and beside the River Bure.

The village of Coltishall, in the Bure Valley, is the starting point for the walk.

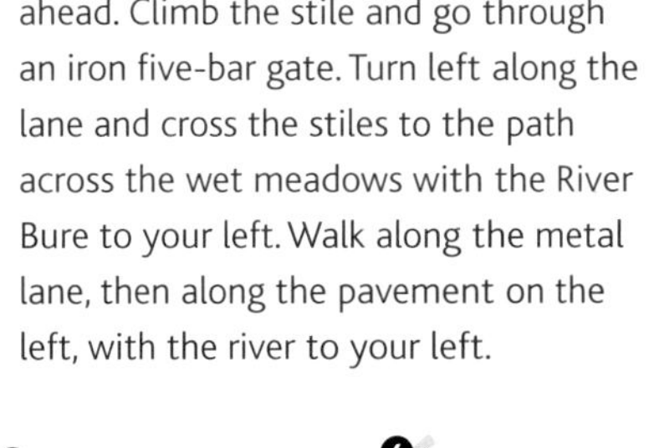

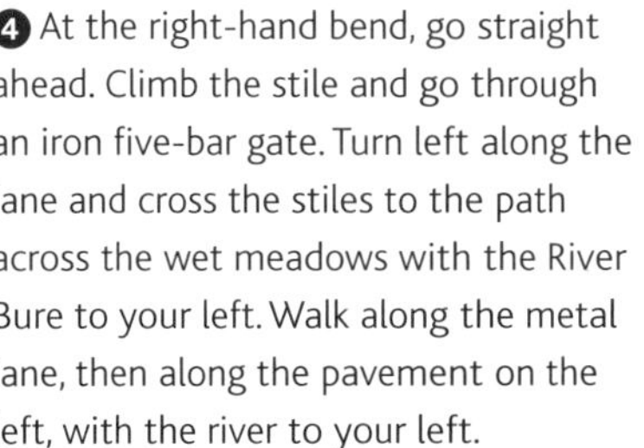

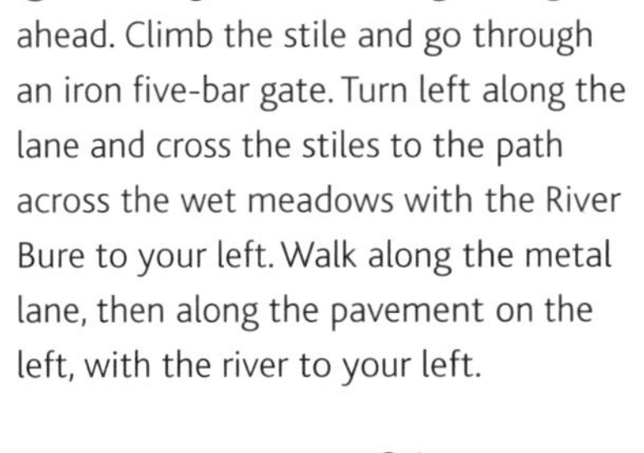

❶ From the car park, go down the steps on to the path. Turn right and follow the path, keeping the railway line on your left. Ignore all the paths that turn off to the right.

❷ With the white house on your left, go through the gate, cross the road and continue along the path opposite. When you reach the bridge, turn right down the steps and go straight ahead – do not turn left under the bridge. Follow the path along the field edge with the hedge on your right, then on your left. At the tree boundary, bear right.

❸ Go through a gap in the hedge and follow the path along the field edge, with the trees on your left. Go through a gap in the hedge and down some steps to the road. Turn right along the main road, then left along Top Road. Take the third turning on the right, signposted 'To the river', and go along The Street.

❹ At the right-hand bend, go straight ahead. Climb the stile and go through an iron five-bar gate. Turn left along the lane and cross the stiles to the path across the wet meadows with the River Bure to your left. Walk along the metal lane, then along the pavement on the left, with the river to your left.

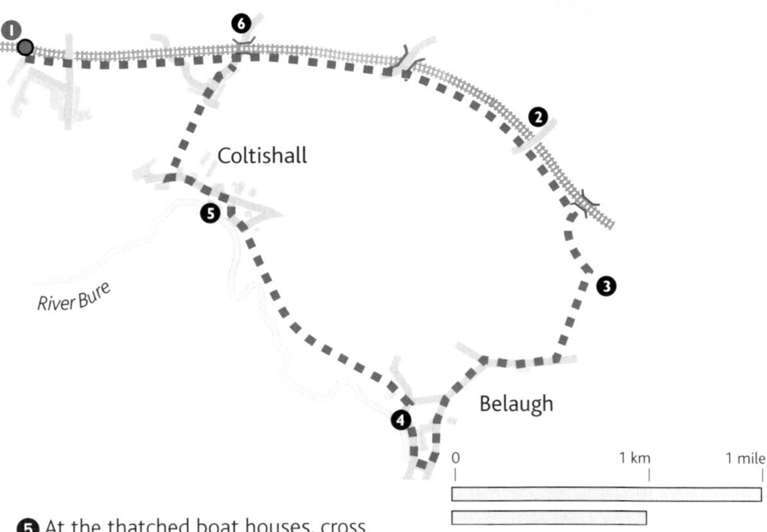

❺ At the thatched boat houses, cross the grass to a path, cross the bridge, and turn right on to the main road. Cross the road to the telephone box and fingerpost. Go along the narrow path and through a kissing gate. When you reach the road, keep straight ahead.

❻ Go up the steps on the left and turn left along the path. Turn left up the steps to return to the car park.

access information

The walk starts at the free car park at the old station which is off Station Road, Coltishall. Coltishall is 13 km north of Norwich on the B1150. For Norfolk Bus routes, Freephone 0500 626116 Monday to Friday 9 a.m. to 5 p.m.

further information

Coltishall is widely known for its air base, where once the famous Second World War pilot, Sir Douglas Bader, was based with 242 Squadron. Evidence of both Roman and Saxon occupation has been found in this area.

▲ Map: Explorer 196
▲ Distance: 12.88 km/8 miles
▲ Walk ID: 1090 B. and A. Sandland

Difficulty rating ●●

Time ●●●

▲ River, Pub, Toilets, Church, Stately Home, National Trust/NTS, Wildlife, Birds, Flowers, Great Views, Restaurant, Tea Shop, Woodland, Ancient Monument

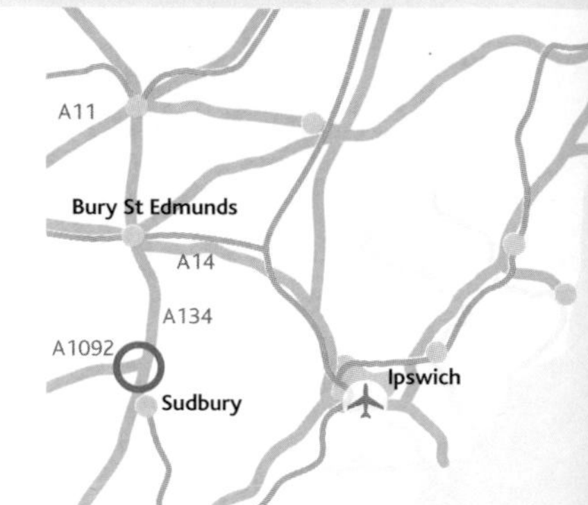

The Stour Valley Way and Glemsford from Long Melford

This walk begins in Long Melford, an idyllic Suffolk village surrounded by sweeping parkland and rolling countryside. There are several great manor houses, including the Tudor Long Melford Hall and the moated Kentwell Hall.

❶ From the car park, turn left. Cross the A1092 to the church. Turn left in the churchyard, go through a gateway, then cross a stile. Turn right across another stile and a paddock. Cross two more stiles, passing woodland to a third stile. Walk across to another stile and turn towards Kentwell Hall. Just before the gates, turn left. Go through two gates, then bear right. Follow the track, passing fields then woodland.

❷ Turn left. Follow the path, with woodland then a ditch and field on your left. When you reach trees ahead and a gap on the left, turn right. Where the track goes left to a farm, carry on and cross a footbridge. Follow the track to the road. Turn right, then left at Mill Farmhouse.

❸ Cross a metal footbridge then turn half right to a bridge over a ditch. Turn right with the ditch on your right. At the end of the field on your left, turn left and walk on to meet Park Lane. Turn left, then turn right along the left side of a field. At the end, turn left along a signposted footpath.

further information

At the National Trust property Kentwell Hall, there are frequent reconstructions of life as it would have been when the house was built in 1564. Authentic clothing is worn, and there are demonstrations of cooking, weaving and spinning in Tudor style.

access information

Long Melford lies slightly north of Sudbury and just west of the A134 from Sudbury to Bury St Edmunds. The walk starts from the free car park opposite Kentwell Hall, and there is plenty of additional parking.

This view of the village of Nayland, in the Stour Valley, has remained unchanged for centuries.

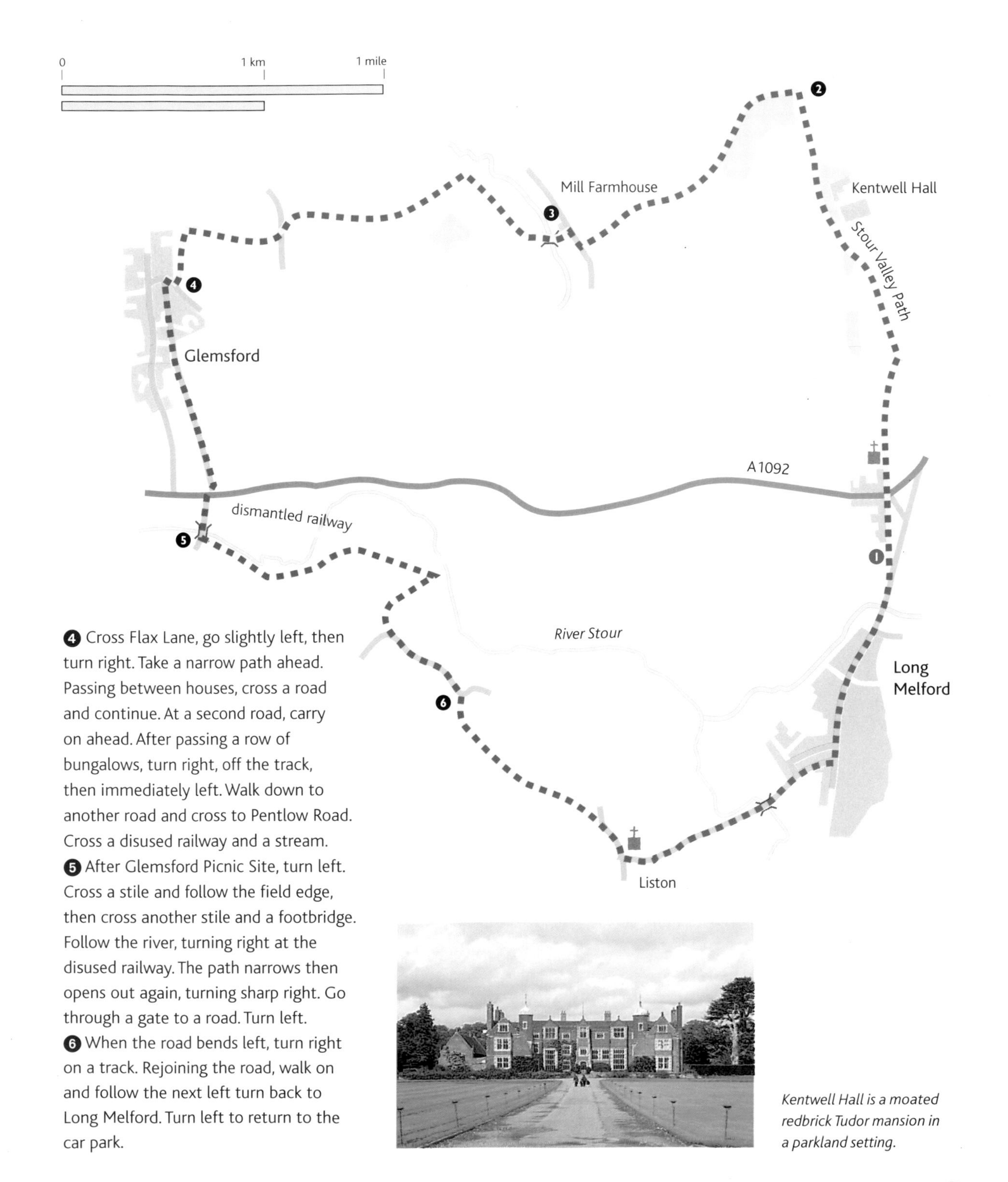

❹ Cross Flax Lane, go slightly left, then turn right. Take a narrow path ahead. Passing between houses, cross a road and continue. At a second road, carry on ahead. After passing a row of bungalows, turn right, off the track, then immediately left. Walk down to another road and cross to Pentlow Road. Cross a disused railway and a stream.

❺ After Glemsford Picnic Site, turn left. Cross a stile and follow the field edge, then cross another stile and a footbridge. Follow the river, turning right at the disused railway. The path narrows then opens out again, turning sharp right. Go through a gate to a road. Turn left.

❻ When the road bends left, turn right on a track. Rejoining the road, walk on and follow the next left turn back to Long Melford. Turn left to return to the car park.

Kentwell Hall is a moated redbrick Tudor mansion in a parkland setting.

▲ Map: Explorer 229 and 230W
▲ Distance: 6.44 km/4 miles
▲ Walk ID: 219 J. and C. Boldero

Difficulty rating ●●

Time ●●

▲ River, Toilets, Wildlife, Birds, Flowers, Good for Wheelchairs

Knettishall Heath Country Park

This walk begins in Knettishall Heath Country Park, the meeting place of Peddars Way, Icknield Way and Angles Way. The route follows the River Little Ouse for a short way, before crossing heathland and running through woodland.

❶ From the entrance to the country park, walk westwards along the track, with the river on your right and the picnic area on your left. Immediately after the toilet block, turn right along the path signed with a blue arrow and three waves. Ignore the path that turns to the left at a bend.

❷ Take the path to the left beside the river and follow it until it turns left away from the river. Cross a bridge, ignoring the path on the left with a blue arrow, and keep straight ahead. At the T-junction, keep right, walking into woodland.

❸ At the next T-junction of tracks, turn left along Peddars Way. Go round the barrier, cross the road, and cross the car park opposite. Go through the open gateway on to the Icknield Way. Carry straight along the path, which narrows between trees.

❹ At the end of the woodland to your left, and at the fingerpost sign, turn left through woodland and continue along the wide path between the crops, which becomes a track. At the end, turn left along a country lane.

❺ Where two roads join, and just after a Suffolk County Council notice, turn left across the grass to a sign 'Horse riders'. Continue along the woodland path. As the path goes downhill, turn right at a post with a sign on the other side, still in the wood.

❻ When the path forks left, take the narrower path straight ahead under trees. At the next T-junction of paths, turn right for a very short distance. Turn left at a yellow arrow marker, still in the wood. Follow the arrows (one is white) through the woods. At the T-junction of paths, turn right, go through the barrier, and cross over to the car park.

access information

There is free parking at Knettishall Heath Country Park, which is situated 9.7 km east of Thetford off the A1066. Follow the 'Country Park' signs along a country lane for about 1.5 km to just beyond the river bridge. For information about public transport, contact Suffolk County Council Travelline on 08459 583358.

further information

The country park is 'wheelchair friendly', with the wheelchair symbol clearly indicated on posts. The heathland is grazed by Exmoor ponies, fallow deer and Hebredian sheep, enabling rare wild flowers to grow, such as dropwort and tormentil, as well as the more common foxglove, gorse, harebell and heather.

The hardy Exmoor pony is one of the best-known residents of this area.

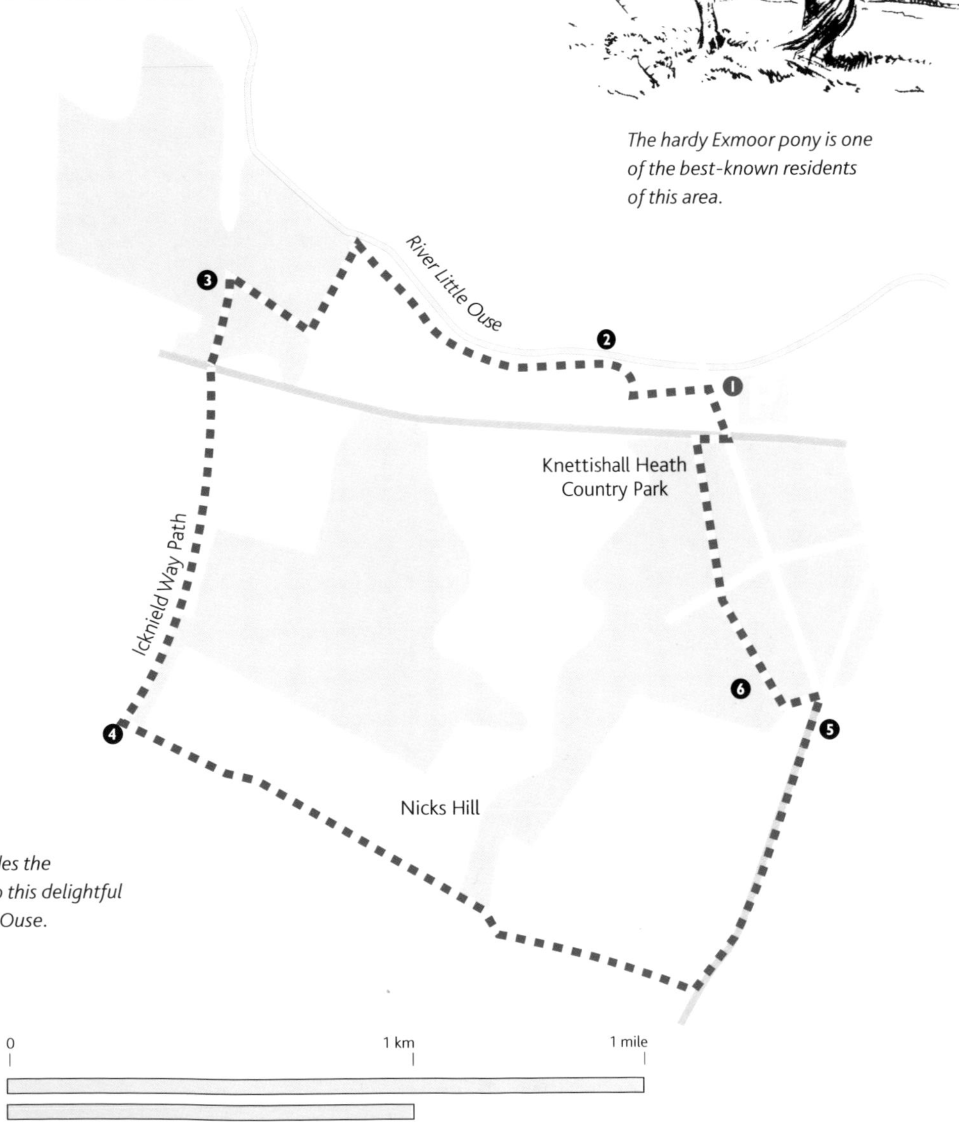

River Little Ouse

Knettishall Heath Country Park

Icknield Way Path

Nicks Hill

A windmill provides the finishing touch to this delightful view of the Little Ouse.

0

1 km

1 mile

▲ Map: Explorer OL 24
▲ Distance: 11 km/6¾ miles
▲ Walk ID: 1041 Barry Smith

Difficulty rating

Time

▲ Hills or Fells, River, Wildlife, Great Views, Moor, Woodland

Gradbach Wood and The Roaches from Gradbach

This is a magnificent walk with plenty of contrast. From Gradbach, you follow the beautiful River Dane and Black Brook, followed by forest paths in deep woodland, before climbing to The Roaches, a rocky moorland ridge.

❶ Turn right out of the car park and fork right to the Youth Hostel. Follow a short lane on the left of the Hostel car park to the corner. Go up the steps and path and climb the stile. The path widens into a farm track. Climb the stile in the wall ahead and turn right downhill to Castors Bridge. Cross the footbridge into Forest Bottom, and follow the sign left.

❷ Continue up the path beside Black Brook and through Gradbach Wood. At the next fork in the path, take the lower one to continue beside, but above, Black Brook. Join a wider path coming from the right, and continue left.

❸ At the top of a hill, take the sign for Roach End over a small stream. Follow the path, mostly uphill, into open countryside. Cross a stile, then another squeeze stile almost immediately on the left leading to a road.

❹ Cross the road and follow the path opposite, uphill and by a wall, on to The Roaches. Climb to the trig point and carry on. At the deep cleft in the ridge on your right, follow a path going down to the next left turn. Follow the path along the base of the cliff to the end.

❺ Ignore the steps to the right and take the path downhill into the col, towards the gate and path leading to Hen Cloud. Ascend Hen Cloud if you wish. If not, turn left and follow the main path straight ahead. After a farm track, you reach a minor road.

❻ Follow the road to the right, then turn left opposite Newstone Farm. At the next junction, bear left, then follow the green lane signposted to Gradbach across the fields. Turn right, passing the fork to the Youth Hostel, and return to the car park.

access information

From Buxton, take the A53 Leek road for about 8 km. At the sign for Flash, turn right on a minor road, bearing left for Gradbach after 0.5 km. In another 3.5 km. turn left, signed for Gradbach Youth Hostel, then turn right into the car park.

The spectacular view from The Roaches is well worth the climb.

further information

This area is rich in myths and legends. There are stories of a headless rider and a tall man dressed in green, which could be folk recollections of the story of Sir Gawain in Arthurian legend. Lud's Church, a cave on The Roaches estate, is said to be the legendary Green Chapel in a 14th-century poem reciting Sir Gawain's story.

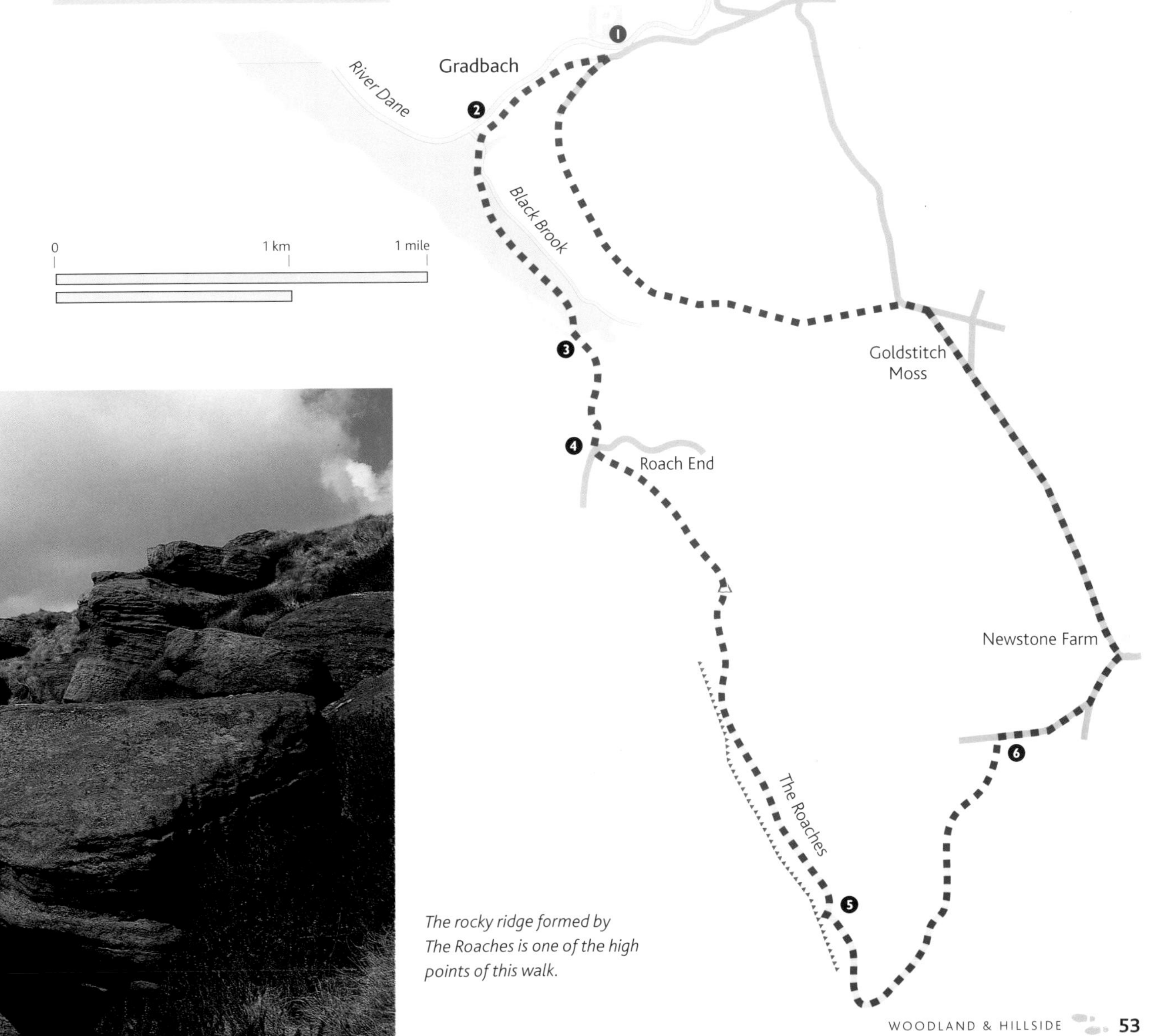

The rocky ridge formed by The Roaches is one of the high points of this walk.

▲ Map: Explorer 206
▲ Distance: 6.44 km/4 miles
▲ Walk ID: 1011 R. and J. Glynn

Difficulty rating

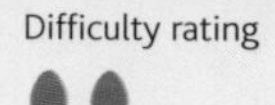

Time

▲ Hills, Lake, Pub, Toilets, Church, Stately Home, Wildlife, Birds, Flowers, Great Views, Butterflies, Food Shop, Woodland

Church Charwelton from Woodford Halse

This simple but rewarding walk is in the midst of lovely rural Northamptonshire agricultural land. It visits the site of the medieval village of Charwelton, with its beautiful little church, before returning along part of the Jurassic Way.

❶ From St Mary the Virgin Church, walk along School Street past the library. Turn left opposite Old Barn on to a hard track that crosses the River Cherwell and climb steps up to the road. Follow the path opposite, through the white barrier rails, and continue between a fence and bushes, then with the hedge on the right only. Keep to the edge of fields over two stiles and look for an oak tree with a sign on it to bear diagonally left.

❷ Follow this sign and head for a gap, to cut off the top corner of the field. Cross the footbridge and walk on. Climb a stile into the next field and follow the hedge on the right, eventually turning right through a metal gate. Follow the fence on the right, turning right with the fence line, then follow the hedge on the right to a stile ahead. Walk across the next field, then bear left to a gap in the hedge. Cross the footbridge, and follow the left-hand field edge.

access information

Woodford Halse lies east of the A361 between Banbury and Daventry. At Byfield, take the road signed to Woodford Halse, drive into the village, and park in the vicinity of the church.

The spire of the medieval Church of St Mary the Virgin in the village of Charwelton dominates the winter landscape.

further information

Unfortunately the church at Charwelton is kept locked, but it is well worth going into the porch and peering through the grids in the door to admire the beautiful interior.

❸ Turn left through a metal gate and cross the medieval village site, bearing right of the farm buildings. Go through two gates to the church. Follow the Jurassic Way marker, bearing right towards the far fence line. Follow the fence to a footbridge and a gate. Bear left towards the railway bridge. Near the bridge, go through a metal gate on to a path, crossing it to continue along the field edges. Go through a wooden gate and walk on uphill.

❹ At the Ramblers' Millennium fingerpost, walk on, following the hard track between woodland and fields. At the end of the track turn left along the road, following the pavement for a short distance. Turn right on to a woodland path, the Jurassic Way, crossing a bridge to turn left into Castle Road. Turn left at the top of the road, and walk back to the church.

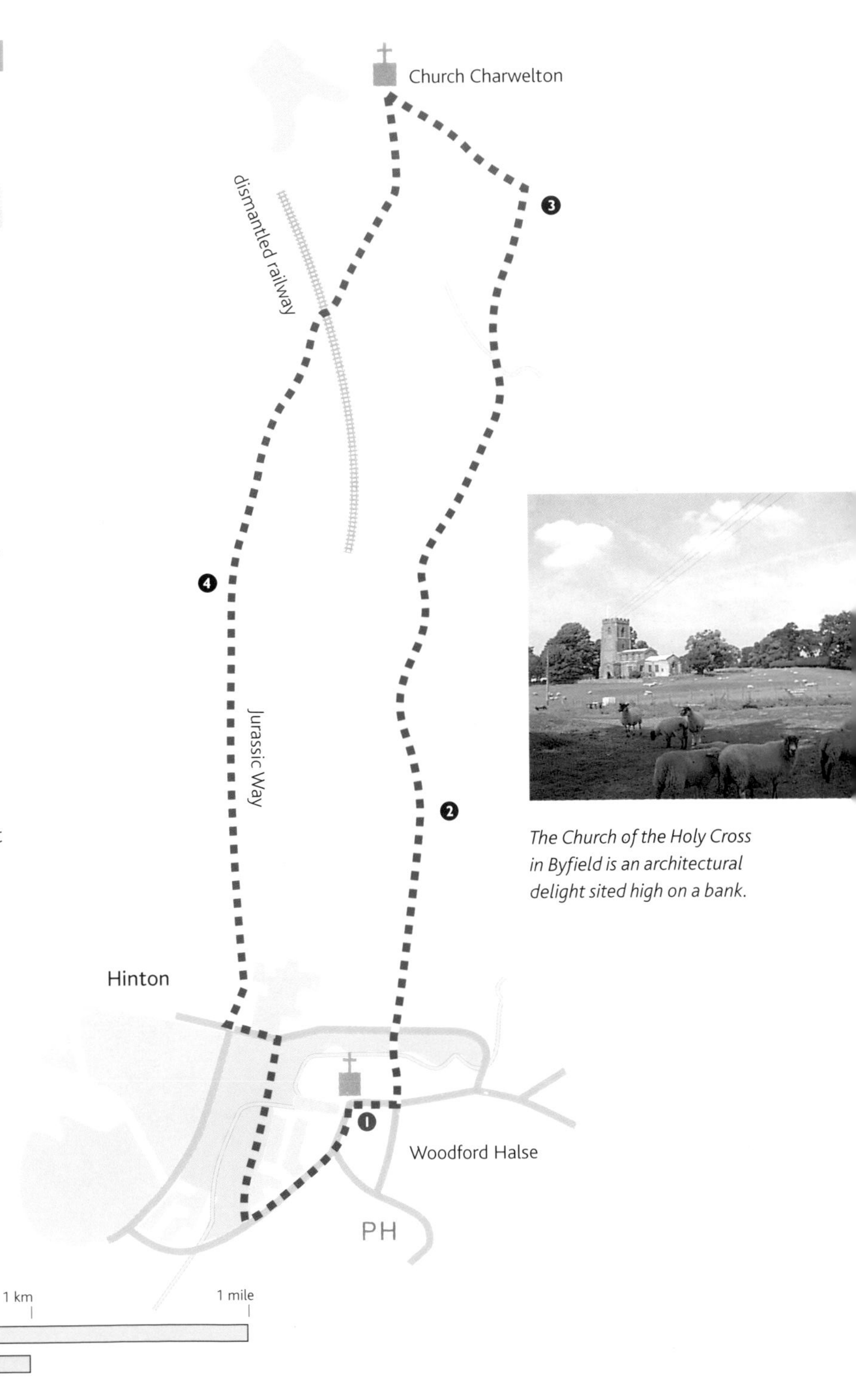

The Church of the Holy Cross in Byfield is an architectural delight sited high on a bank.

▲ Map: Explorer 180
▲ Distance: 12.08 km/7½ miles
▲ Walk ID: 1181 R. and J. Glynn

Difficulty rating

Time

▲ River, Lake, Pub, Toilets, Church, Wildlife, Birds, Flowers, Great Views, Food Shop, Woodland, Ancient Monument

Finstock from Charlbury

This walk on the edge of the Cotswolds follows lanes, bridleways and footpaths through beautiful surroundings. The route encircles the Cornbury Estate, on part of the Oxfordshire Way, edges the Wychwood Forest, and returns via Cornbury Park.

❶ From the car park, turn right opposite the fountain and walk along Browns Lane, passing the Bull Inn. Turn right and walk down the road past the Library and Post Office. Turn left past the Chapel on Dyers Hill and walk on, over the river, past the station and over a road bridge.

❷ Turn right on a bridleway signed to Walcot and follow the path past Cotswold stone cottages, Top Barn (further on), then uphill and downhill. Turn left on a minor road called Catsham Lane.

❸ At the next junction, follow the road opposite along the edge of Wychwood Forest, signed to Leafield. Pass Ranger's Lodge, staying on the road at the entrance to Cornbury Park, and walk with woodland on either side. Turn left opposite Watermans Farm and follow the sign on to a woodland path.

❹ Come out in a clearing and turn right to join a track which passes some old huts. The path drops down to a lake and turns left by a metal gate and a fence. Climb up Patch Hill through woodland, to a clearing. Continue along the edge of the wood and come out in meadowland.

❺ Turn left along the Witney road through Finstock and beyond, then turn left to follow a bridleway signed to Cornbury Park Fishery. Cross the bridge over the lake and take the right of two gates ahead. Passing South Hill Lodge, follow the fence line of Cornbury Park.

❻ Go through a wooden gate and turn right between the pillars of a wide river bridge. Cross a smaller railway bridge later on. At North Lodge Gate, turn left into Charlbury. Passing St Mary's Church, follow the road to the Bell Inn in Church Street. At the junction, cross the road and walk back to the start.

The Church of St Mary at Charlbury is a typical Cotswold church, built of grey stone with an imposing square tower.

This tree-lined walk has a warm, golden beauty in the dying days of autumn.

access information

Charlbury is at the crossroads of the B4437 and the B4022 just north of Witney. Free car parking is available at the Spendlove Centre in the village, where the walk starts.

further information

Peace and tranquillity prevail in this area of outstanding natural beauty. The woodland path through part of the Wychwood Forest is magical, with mature trees giving refuge to many different birds species, while Cornbury Park is spectacular with its herd of deer roaming freely through the majestic trees.

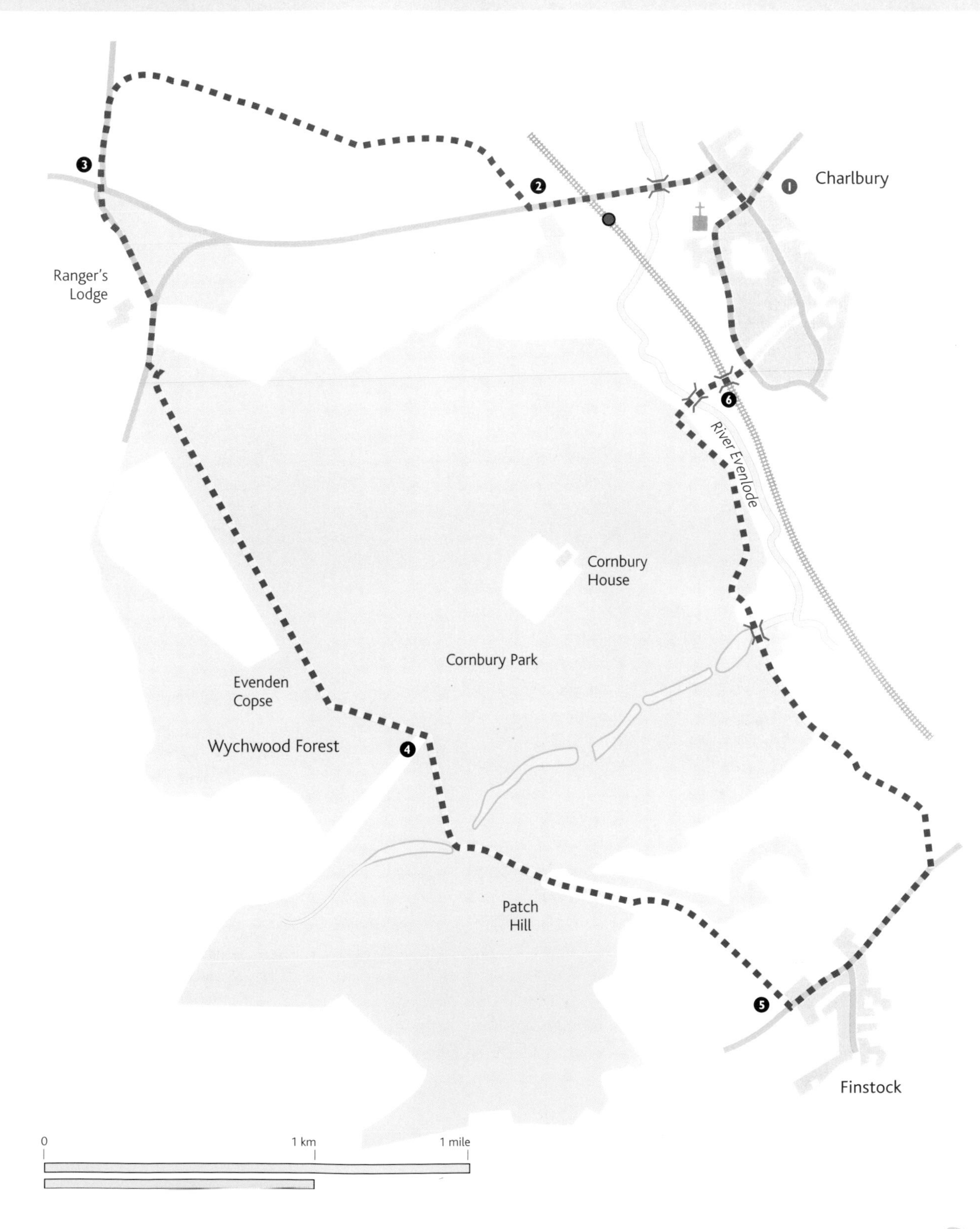
Charlbury
Ranger's Lodge
River Evenlode
Cornbury House
Cornbury Park
Evenden Copse
Wychwood Forest
Patch Hill
Finstock
0
1 km
1 mile

▲ Map: LRM 151, EXP 191W, TRM 6, TRM 9
▲ Distance: 7.65 km/4¾ miles
▲ Walk ID: 523 R. and J. Glynn

Difficulty rating

Time

▲ Parkland, Castle, Moat, Church, Fulling Mill, Stream, Great Views

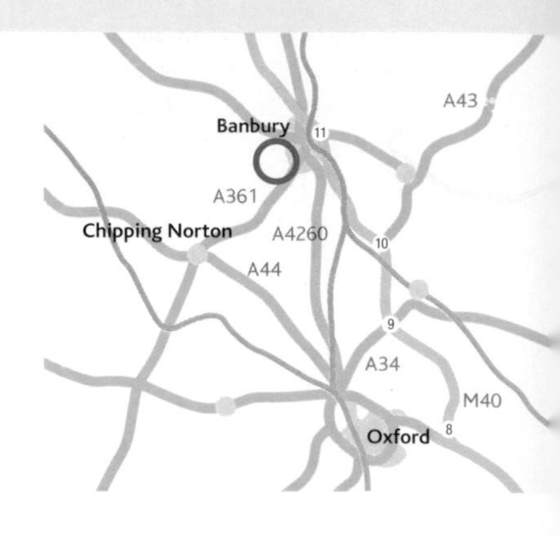

Lower Tadmarton from Broughton

This walk starts in the grounds of Broughton Castle, with a splendid view of this fairy-tale moated castle and the delightful church beside it. You also pass a fulling mill, a legacy of the days when plush weaving was a flourishing local industry.

❶ Just within the castle entrance, climb a stone stile, following the left-hand path. Walk uphill over parkland with the castle and moat on your left. At the brow of the hill, bear right towards a copse. Walk to the right of the copse towards a stile.

❷ Cross the stile and walk with the fence on your left. Turn left over two stiles, passing some farm buildings, and walk with the fence and a hedge on your right, across two fields. Go through a metal gate and turn left. Walk down past the fulling mill.

❸ Go through a metal gate and turn left to a tree on the bank. Go through another gate and walk across two fields. Go through a wide gap into the next field and head diagonally right. Go through the gap in a hedge and follow the hedge on your right for a short distance.

❹ Take the narrow path to the right, walking between a hedge and a copse. Carry on to a metal gate leading through a kennels, and follow the track to the road. Turn left and walk to the main road junction. Cross and turn left again.

❺ Turn right towards Bloxham. After Oak Tree Farm, turn left on a bridleway. Go through a walkers' gate, now with a spinney on your right. Go through the second metal gate on the left and the walkers' gate immediately on the right, and follow the path with Nayland Farm on your right. Stay on the path around two field edges.

❻ Go through a walkers' gate to the main road. Turn right and walk towards Broughton. Just before a house, turn left on a stone path leading to Broughton Church, crossing the footbridge into the churchyard. Leave by the wooden gate and follow the drive back to the start.

access information

Broughton is on the B4035 just south-west of Banbury. Park on a small lay-by adjacent to the main entrance to Broughton Castle.

The Oxfordshire countryside is a tranquil landscape for walkers.

further information

Broughton Castle and Church date back to the 14th and 15th century. The castle is occupied by Lord Saye and Sele, a descendant of William Fiennes, a prominent figure in the Civil War and an ancestor of the famous Fiennes family. The castle has limited opening to the public.

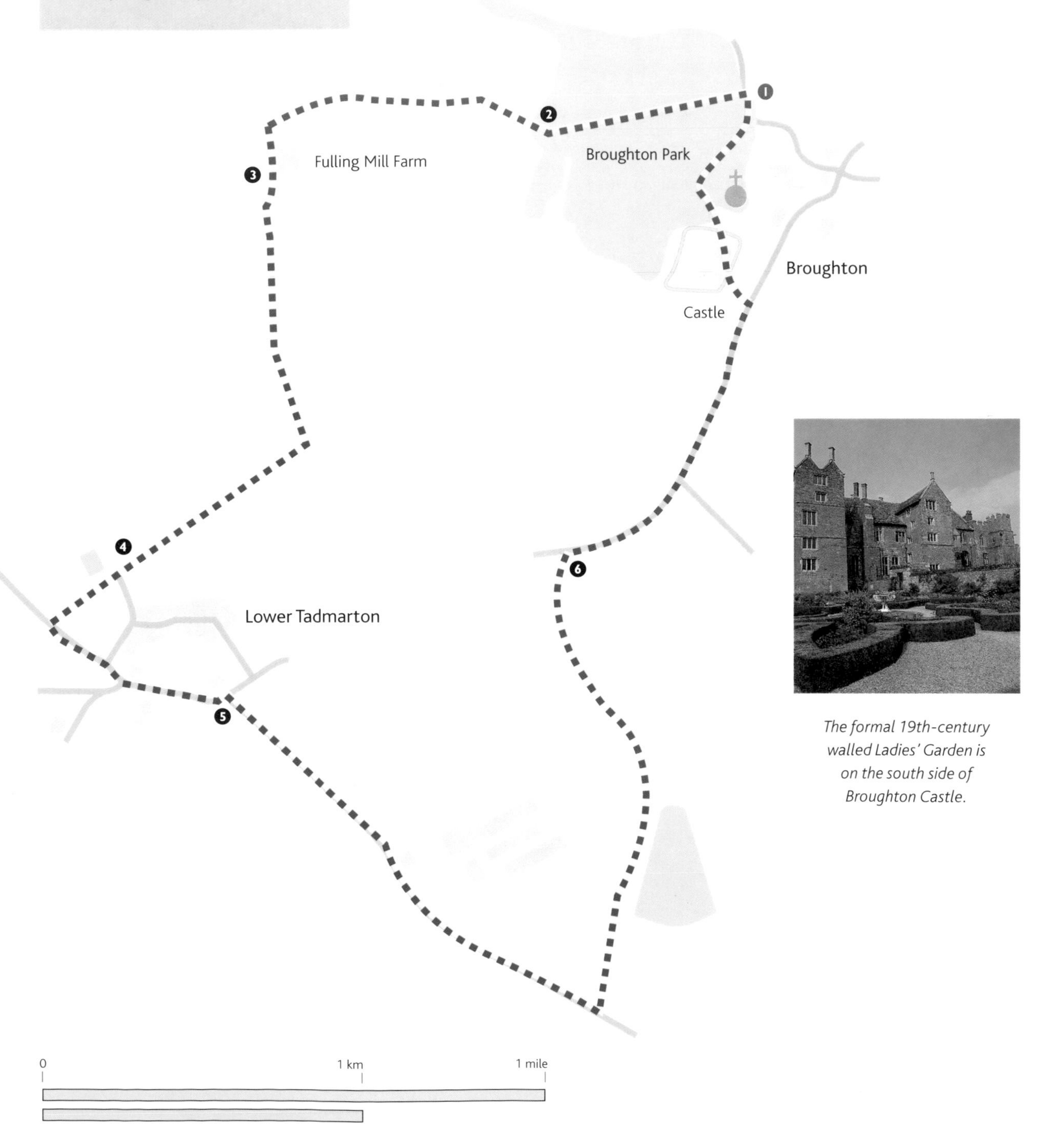

The formal 19th-century walled Ladies' Garden is on the south side of Broughton Castle.

▲ Map: Explorer 271
▲ Distance: 9.66 km/6 miles
▲ Walk ID: 1440 David Berry

Difficulty rating

Time

▲ Pub, Toilets, Museum, Church, Wildlife, Great Views

Laxton from Egmanton

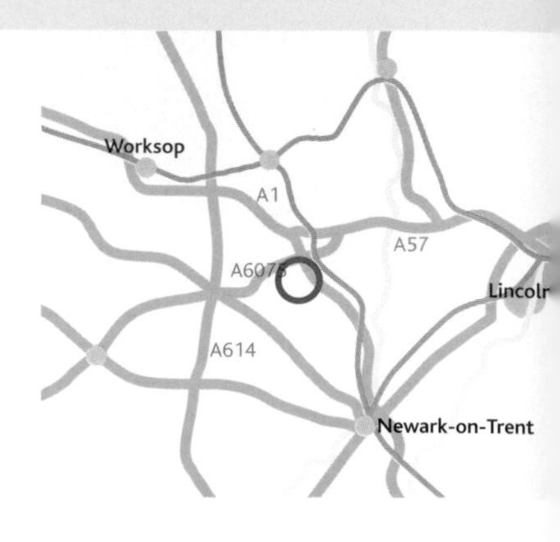

From Egmanton, this walk initially climbs gently on farm tracks before taking to field footpaths leading to Laxton and a circular return to the start. Laxton is England's last open field farming village with an ancient strip field system.

❶ From the Old Plough Inn, turn right. Fork right along Weston Road, then turn right up Wood Lane, which becomes a stone track. Follow the track to skirt the edge of Egmanton Wood. When the track ends, continue ahead on a path across a field to a hedge, and turn left.

❷ Go through a gap in the hedge, turn left and follow the field edge. Turn right to follow the footpath, which has an electricity pole and two large trees on it, to the far side of the field. Go through a gateway and turn right along a track.

❸ Turn left and follow the footpath to a playing field. Go past the pavilion and through the hedge. Turn right, then left through the hedge and under a wooden bar. Cross the field diagonally to a footpath sign. Follow the left edge of the next field to a stile. Follow the footpath to the road and turn right through Laxton.

❹ Fork right along the 'No Through Road'. By a bungalow, turn right, following the footpath across the field to the left, then to the corner. Climb the stile and go through the gateway beyond. Walk down this field to climb a stile on the left, then follow the hedge, turning left at the ditch. Cross a footbridge and a stile.

❺ Follow the path ahead. Where the path diverges from the hedge on your right, head towards a communications tower. When the path ends, climb the mound and turn right along a track for a short distance. Go through a gateway, but follow the tractor tracks parallel to the hedge instead of the yellow arrow.

❻ As the track goes downhill, follow the footpath proper to a fingerpost in the far hedge. Climb the stile, turn right and follow the fence. In the right-hand corner, climb the stile and follow a straight line, keeping the hedge on your left. At the last field, go through the gate to a short track, then turn right to Egmanton.

further information

At Step 5/6, there is a yellow arrow across a field, apparently indicating the direction of the footpath across the crop. However, previous walkers have followed tractor tracks which run parallel to the hedge and about 30 m into the field, bending to the left and then curving right with the hedge.

access information

Egmanton lies between the A6075 Ollerton to Tuxford road and the A616 Newark to Ollerton road. It is only a short distance off the A1 – northbound, leave at Tuxford, southbound, leave at Markham Moor. Car parking is available on the village roads.

There are bus services to Egmanton village from Tuxford, Newark, Ollerton and Retford.

Laxton parish church, with its mellow walls and overgrown graveyard, has a timeless air.

This view of the renowned strip farming of England's last medieval open field system at Laxton is one of the main points of historic interest in this area.

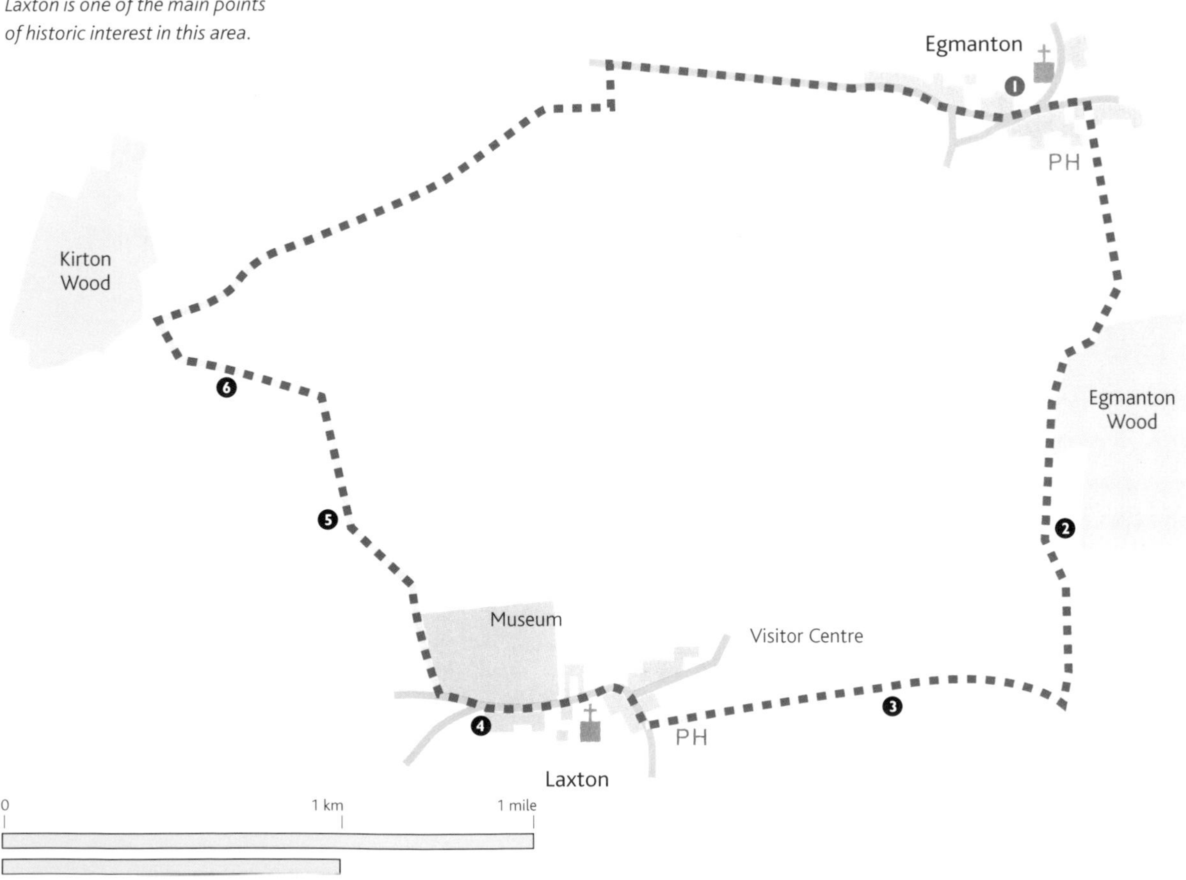

▲ Map: Explorer 205
▲ Distance: 8 km/5 miles
▲ Walk ID: 1431 Wendy Pickler

Difficulty rating

Time

▲ River, Pub, Toilets, Church, Café, Public Transport

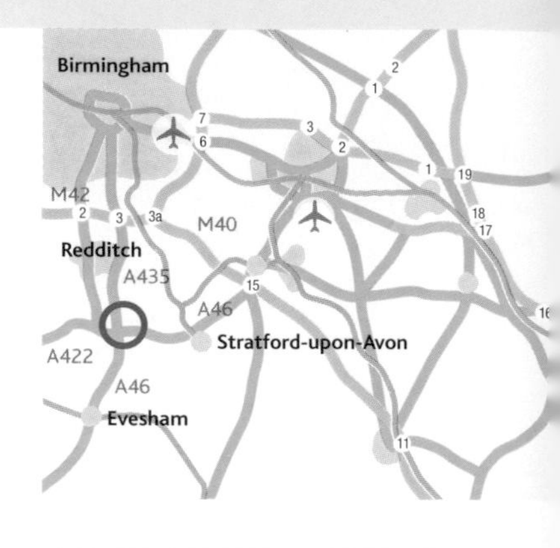

Oversley and Exhall from Alcester

This short walk begins in the old Roman town of Alcester (Alauna) and meets up with both the Arden and the Heart of England Way. The route touches the pretty village of Exhall before climbing up to pass by Oversley Castle.

❶ From the church, turn left. Cross over to walk down Malt Mill Lane, bearing right, then taking a left-hand path across a green. Cross the main road and follow signs for the Arden Way and Heart of England Way. At Oversley Green, cross the river and bear left. Look for a footpath sign on the right soon after passing 'Polkerris' on the left.

❷ Climb the stile. Cross the field diagonally right, then another stile, and pass a golf driving range. Go through a gate, following the left-hand field edge. Turn right at the corner. Go through another gate. Follow the track to a gate and stile. Carry on through two more gates to a lane. Turn right and go under the bridge.

❸ Bear left and climb a stile by a gate, following a waymark track beside the wood. Go through a gateway, keeping ahead along the track. Go through a gate and keep ahead, with a hedge on the left. Go through another gate, with the hedge on the right. Go through two more gates and a farmyard to the road.

❹ Turn right, then immediately right again on a tarmac track. After Rosehall Farm go through a gate to a track. Go through another gateway to reach Oversley Wood. Turn left, following signs for the Arden Way. As the Arden Way turns right, leave it by keeping on ahead.

❺ At a T-junction below Oversley Castle, turn right towards Primrose Hill. Just past the two silos on top, follow the track right and down the hill, across a stile on the left and over the bypass on the pedestrian bridge. Follow Primrose Lane to a T-junction and turn left.

❻ By the caravan park, follow a footpath sign on the left to a path on the right. Cross the footbridge over the river. Carry on until you come out opposite the High Street, then return to the church.

access information

Alcester lies some 13 km north of Stratford-upon-Avon, and the town centre is well signposted from all directions. Park in the free car park behind the Swan pub, which is along the old main Stratford road, not far from the small roundabout with a metal globe in the middle.

This black-and-white half-timbered building is a relatively modern one in the ancient Roman town of Alcester.

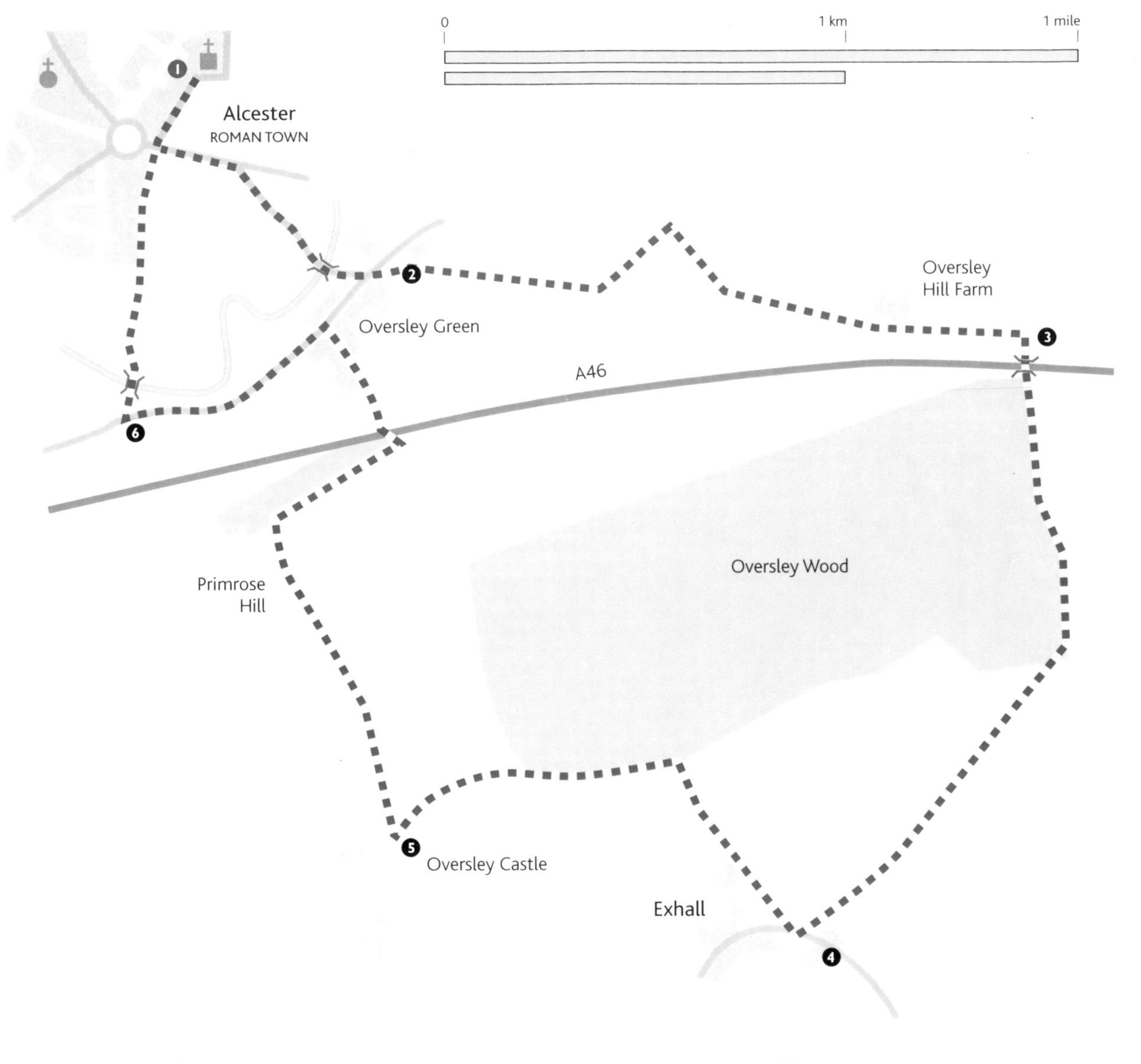

further information

The walk gives views of Ragley Hall, the home of the Marquis and Marchioness of Hartford. The house is open to the public.

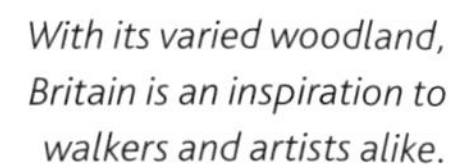

With its varied woodland, Britain is an inspiration to walkers and artists alike.

Index

acknowledgements

The publishers wish to thank the following for the use of their pictures:
Joy & Charles Boldero: p.47; Collections: pp.16 Liz Starrs, 22 Robin Weaver, 28 Yuri Lewinski, 29 Alan Barnes, 40 Robin Weaver, 46 George Wright, 52/3 + 53 Robin Weaver, 54 David McGill, 58 David McGill, 59 Yuri Lewinski, 62 Colin Underhill; Corbis: pp.8 + 10 Roger Tidman, 12/3 Robert Estall, 14/5 David Hoskins, 8 Michael Boys, 19 John Heseltine, 20/1 Bryan Pickering/Eye Ubiquitous, 25 Jason Hawkes, 26/7 Greenhalf Photography, 30 Annie Griffiths Belt, 32 + 33 Chris Andrews, 34 Colin Garratt/Milepost, 35 Buddy Mays, 37 Robert Estall, 42 + 43 Michael S Yamashita, 48 + 50 Robert Estall, 56L Ric Ergenbright, 60 Robert Holmes, 61 Michael St. Maur Sheil; Ron & Jenny Glynn: pp.27, 55, 56R; Jim Grindle: p.41; Steward Howat: pp.23, 39.